3 1994 01513 2217

2/14

SANT  P9-AFZ-538

THE HOMEGROWN PRESCHOOLER

BY KATHY H. LEE AND LESLI M. RICHARDS

DEDICATION

This book is dedicated to Mrs. Diana Risher, who first taught me to write down my thoughts, and to the many women who showed me how to live at home. Thank you, Mom, Cindy, Debbie A., Suzanne, Debbie M., Susan, and my sweet Aunt Nell.

—Kathy

This book is dedicated to my aunt Bobbie Verges, whose love for children, education, and homemaking
was quietly watched by a little girl whose biggest wish was to be just like her;
and to God, who showed me that Auntie Bobbie's home was different because He was there.

—Lesli

ACKNOWLEDGEMENTS

How could I write this book without my seven blessings and my amazing husband?
They are the realization of my childhood hopes and dreams.
MaryAnn Kohl has been a dear friend and mentor for many years. Thank you, MaryAnn.
Bev Bos has inspired me to think out of the box with young children and to always be willing to turn on the water hose.
My dear friend Rachel Pate has challenged me to be the best me possible.
I will forever be grateful for her gentle nudges along the way.
Christy Montes, thank you for keeping me well in body and in mind.

—Kathy

I certainly do not deserve my husband, who tirelessly works to make all of my dreams come true, lovingly leads our five children, and whips up sensory tables and easels and whatever else I dream up in his workshop!
Rebecca, my oldest, volunteered much time caring for her siblings while I wrote.
And my other children were so understanding of deadlines and long days. This truly was a family effort!
Thank you, Mom, for taking up the slack for me while I wrote and for rescuing me
from computer problems during deadline week!
Thank you also to Vicki Miller for your encouragement, prayers, and friendship.
And thank you to Cyndy Roache for always spurring me on by your creative example.

—Lesli

THE HOMEGROWN PRESCHOOLER
Teaching Your Kids in the Places They Live

KATHY H. LEE & LESLI M. RICHARDS

GRYPHON HOUSE, INC.
LEWISVILLE, NC

● PARENT 649.68 LEE
Lee, Kathy H.
The homegrown preschooler

$29.95
CENTRAL   31994015132217

COPYRIGHT

©2013 Kathy H. Lee and Lesli M. Richards

Published by Gryphon House, Inc.
P. O. Box 10, Lewisville, NC 27023
800.638.0928; 877.638.7576 (fax)
Visit us on the web at www.gryphonhouse.com.

All rights reserved. No part of this publication may be reproduced or transmitted in any form or by any means, electronic or technical, including photocopy, recording, or any information storage or retrieval system, without prior written permission of the publisher. Printed in the USA. Every effort has been made to locate copyright and permission information.

Cover photographs courtesy of Dawn Camp, Avery Kronz, and Abigail Akins

LIBRARY OF CONGRESS CATALOGING-IN-PUBLICATION DATA

Lee, Kathy H., 1968-
 The homegrown preschooler : teaching your kids in the places they live / by Kathy H. Lee and Lesli M. Richards.
    p. cm.
 Includes index.
 ISBN 978-0-87659-451-3
 1. Home schooling. I. Richards, Lesli M. II. Title.
 LC40.L44 2013
 649'.68--dc23
                    2012047844

BULK PURCHASE

Gryphon House books are available for special premiums and sales promotions as well as for fund-raising use. Special editions or book excerpts also can be created to specifications. For details, contact the Director of Marketing at Gryphon House.

DISCLAIMER

Gryphon House, Inc. cannot be held responsible for damage, mishap, or injury incurred during the use of or because of activities in this book. Appropriate and reasonable caution and adult supervision of children involved in activities and corresponding to the age and capability of each child involved is recommended at all times. Do not leave children unattended at any time. Observe safety and caution at all times.

TABLE OF CONTENTS

INTRODUCTION
OUR JOURNEYS TO GROWING OUR CHILDREN AT HOME

KATHY'S JOURNEY

As a little girl I had one dream: to be a mom. As a teenager I had one main job: babysitting. As a college student I had one major: child development. As a career woman I had one career: early childhood. Do you see a pattern? I love children; I always have. To this day, I find great pleasure in hanging out with two- and three-year-olds, listening to them tell me stories and ask me question after question. I do have one small confession: Although I love everyone's children, I love mine more. On June 22, 1996, my world changed forever—I became a mom to a nine-month-old boy. Suddenly, my world of early childhood and motherhood collided.

Before I was married, I had decided that I would one day homeschool my children. I knew several homeschool families and had witnessed the benefits of this method of education. Thankfully, my husband desired the same for our family. I planned on educating our son at home; however, I had grown to love the world of early childhood education. I wanted our son to have the same great experiences that I had taught about, had even written books about. After much deliberation, we decided to enroll our son in preschool.

It was a great experience for him, for the 15 minutes he attended. Yep, he lasted (okay, I lasted) 15 minutes. The moment I walked away from that classroom, I began to question my decision. I was sad that those teachers would witness my son's a-ha moments. I was getting mad at the thought of those teachers reading him stories, watching him play dress-up, or making fly guts with him (more about fly guts later). I wanted to do those things. *I* wanted to make fly guts with

my son. I went back to the classroom, checked out my son from school, and never looked back. We went home and lived! We played! We dressed up! We read! And, we made fly guts!

Now, we have seven children who are all being grown at home. Over the 17 years of schooling, we have made great memories, and we have all learned. As my oldest approaches high school graduation, I now know firsthand how strong the foundation of learning through play is. Children who experience their preschool years discovering and experiencing are more willing to take risks later in their education journey. I am thankful that I have been able to incorporate my love for early childhood education into my homeschool world, and although it hasn't been perfect, it has been an amazing ride!

LESLI'S JOURNEY

Although Kathy and I have much in common, my choice to homeschool was born of very different circumstances. I consider myself an unlikely homeschool mom, especially for preschoolers! While Kathy was born to teach preschoolers and enjoys them immensely, I'm more comfortable with babies and kids who can read. Toddlers can be stubborn and unpredictable, and I bring enough of those qualities to the home already!

I can remember, years ago, talking doubtfully to a friend who had just made the choice to homeschool and thinking she was going to get weird and bake bread and wear denim jumpers to the gym. I enrolled my daughter in preschool at the earliest possible moment! I enjoyed my "me time" while she was at school. I could shop, clean my house, and play with my new baby boy. Why would anyone want to give up that little bit of freedom? I even paid extra for the after-school program.

My world changed drastically in the summer of 2002. After a whirlwind of medical appointments, MRIs, neurological consultations, and long nights of Internet research and pacing the floor, we had our diagnosis and prognosis: autism. With cold, professional detachment, the doctors said our precious, once-smiling, happy baby boy would never speak and would probably live in an institution by the age of 10. Our pediatrician gave us no hope of improvement, and he advised us to start saving for our son's future care after we are gone.

I cannot begin to tell you what havoc such a diagnosis brings to a family. I am thankful for a friend who was only a few months ahead of me on the autism journey; she fought hard to bring me out of the shock and grief and encouraged me to do battle for my little boy. In those years, there was no medical coverage for autism in the state we lived in, and we had to fight for every bit of therapy and care our son received. We found an applied behavior analysis (ABA) program and spent 25 hours a week learning with him at a wonderful child development center. We put him on a gluten-free diet, and within a month we noticed significant improvement. This success spurred me on to find more help for him.

When an opportunity came for my husband to take a new position in Georgia, we jumped at the chance. In California, where we were living, autism was deemed a developmental delay, and we struggled getting insurance to cover our son's care. The laws in Georgia were more favorable, so I was very excited that we would have many more options for Luke. After settling in, I found that the reality was that there was a 17-month wait for a spot for speech and physical therapy, unless we could be very flexible in the time slots. We made the decision to educate our daughter at home for a year, until we could get a better appointment time for our son's therapy. This was going to be a temporary thing.

Fast forward eight years, and here I am. I just spent my summer travelling around Georgia speaking on classical education in the home, and I am a regular speaker at our state and regional homeschool conferences. What started out as a desperate move turned into a year of tea parties and reading aloud to a delightful first grader. I grew in patience and confidence as I taught my daughter, and she blossomed at home. Much to my surprise, I was a natural teacher! When my son's special education placement became undesirable, we brought him home as well. I am happy to report that, at age 11, he has exceeded every medical and educational prognosis. He is doing grade-level work and does far better than he would in a typical classroom.

We have since added three more children to our family mix and have quite a busy homeschool! I have now educated three preschoolers at home and find myself teaching our five children, including one in high school. As my great-grandmother might have said, "Who would have thunk it?"

Not everyone has an inborn desire to school their children at home. Like me, you may feel forced to homeschool by circumstances out of your control, whether they be financial, environmental, or health related. And like me, you may be surprised at what my husband calls "the gifts the monster brought." Like me, you might buy desks and a flag, in an attempt to bring school home, only to abandon those props in favor of a life of reading great books on the couch, fingerpainting on the windows, and spending lots of time outdoors.

We quickly realized that life was school, and while structure is certainly necessary, much of learning can be done within the everyday rhythm of life—measuring flour, skip counting on the trampoline, bringing a meal to a shut-in, writing letters to friends, participating in interesting conversations about big ideas. This truly is a lovely life, one that I never would have expected.

You don't have to be perfect to teach your preschooler at home. You just need to be willing to slow down a bit and see the world through your child's eyes. It's a beautiful view!

Using This Book

This book has two sections. The first half will help you evaluate your priorities and goals for your child and family. It will also paint a picture of what life will look like as you embark on this new adventure. We have included sections on organizing your home environment to maximize the educational impact, along with stories and helpful tips from our years of experience in early childhood education and motherhood. We even address the seasons in life and the unusual circumstances that many families face, such as adoption, pregnancy, or children who have special needs or are chronically ill.

The second half is jam-packed with developmentally appropriate activities that will give your child a firm foundation for lifelong learning. We have divided the activities into target areas of growth that are necessary for healthy and happy preschoolers to be ready for kindergarten in any setting. Using the handy weekly activity checklist, you will be able to choose activities from among the following subjects to make sure that your preschooler is learning across all the developmental domains: home life, science, gross motor, fine motor, math, language and emergent literacy, art, music, and social-emotional.

Because you also need to juggle other responsibilities along with teaching, we have included organization and housekeeping tips, recipes, and sample schedules. Additionally, we have designed a light and sensory table and a Plexiglas easel and have included easy-to-follow plans for those who wish to build their own. Finally, we have included a comprehensive resource list of furniture, storage, and educational supply retailers; sources for children's books and educational resources; and our favorite books, websites, and blogs.

Chapter 1

HOME-SCHOOLING

HARVESTING A BOUNTIFUL LIFE

We think that gardening is a perfect metaphor for homeschooling preschoolers. When you plant a garden, you decide what you want to harvest, then you plan in order to make that vision a reality. Educating your child at home is similar: You consider the learning style and unique talents and interests of your preschooler as you design an educational program just for him. You choose from among the best of curricula, art supplies, music, parks, museums, and enrichment classes to plant in your child the seeds of learning. Teaching your child at home for the preschool years can be full of benefits for your child and your entire family.

In our families, our children have benefited from spending their preschool years in the home. We have been able to provide a custom-tailored education for each of our children. For example, one of Lesli's daughters seemed to

There is a garden in every childhood, an enchanted place where colors are brighter, the air softer, and the morning more fragrant than ever again.

—ELIZABETH LAWRENCE,
author, gardener, and landscape architect

respond well to sensory play; she learned to match upper and lowercase letters by putting a magnetic set of letters into a sensory table of colored rice. One of Kathy's sons spent most of his preschool years dressing up in costumes and dictating stories. Both of these children learned their ABCs and 123s, but we were able to teach them in the manner in which they learned best. A custom-designed education and a low child-to-teacher ratio are something many families pay hefty tuitions to get!

By choosing to homeschool your preschool-age child, you offer him social and emotional benefits. He will have more bonding time with family and will grow closer to his siblings. Your child will have opportunities to learn to express himself emotionally in a safe environment where he knows he will receive unconditional love. By organizing playdates with companions your child's age, you can provide opportunities to learn social skills such as sharing, cooperating, and taking turns. If you are fortunate enough to have extended family living close by, grandparents or other family members can participate in your child's learning. Lesli's mom lives nearby, and she loves taking Lesli's preschooler for the day. They bake, create art, and sing songs. Lesli's mom is happy to integrate any theme or skill Lesli and her daughter are working on. It has been beautiful to watch the baby in a large family being doted on and to see a grandmother reliving her younger days!

When you teach your child at home, the world is your playground, full of opportunities for developing your child's gross motor skills. Together, you can walk trails, climb rocks, turn somersaults, or skip down the sidewalk to the grocery store. Some children need to expel more physical energy than others in order to be able to concentrate on a task. Schooling at home is perfect for those high-energy children.

The flexibility of homeschooling can benefit your entire family. The slower pace lowers the family stress level. You can modify the schedule to best suit your family's needs. For example, Kathy's husband is an accountant who often works late hours during certain seasons. Kathy arranges for family time to be in the morning, and she does more schooling in the afternoons and evenings of those seasons. If a parent travels, the whole family can go. We know families who have followed a travelling parent all over the country, visiting landmarks and museums while still keeping up with their schoolwork. Using box and bag activities, preschool can be easily taken on the road!

A family who learns together grows together. For us, homeschooling has strengthened our families' cohesiveness. As we have taught our children, they have become natural teachers themselves. Even our preschoolers are eager to teach the baby! We enjoy working together on projects. When our older children study history, we capture their studies as opportunities for our preschoolers, by providing information, crafts, and costumes on their developmental level. For example, while our older ones were studying Egypt, we provided plastic Egyptian people and buildings and a bin of sand for open-ended play for the preschoolers. When we studied Greece and India, our preschoolers loved dressing up in costumes. Even if your older children are in a traditional school setting, this a great way for your preschooler to feel a part of her siblings' lives and to look forward to what is coming next!

While the reasons a person may choose the homeschooling path are myriad, the rewards are just as numerous. You will find that you will grow personally through this experience. You have an opportunity to model your love of learning for your child, and you will learn to live more deeply and to pay more attention to detail—admirable and rare endeavors in our hurried world.

In taking on the responsibility of educating our children at home, we, too, have been challenged to learn. We have read up on the latest in early childhood education, learning about child development, learning styles, and educational domains. We have had the joy of discovering alongside our children, of fingerpainting and studying bugs, of witnessing the "a-ha" moments. The preschool years pass quickly, and we have loved experiencing those precious days with our children.

Through networking with other homeschooling families, we have found many social opportunities at co-ops, field trips, and park days. We have made friends and have been able to share ideas, approaches, and successes. We support each other through tough times and challenges such as illness, financial stress, or family crisis.

As you begin to plan for preschool at home, you will need to think about what type of little personality you are dealing with and must strive to allow your child to use her natural abilities to do extraordinary things, while pushing her to grow in areas that do not come as easily. What are your child's natural abilities? What are some more challenging areas in which she has room to grow? No one else knows your child as well as you do. Use your knowledge to formulate a custom educational plan to meet your child's individual educational needs. You are uniquely qualified for this task!

As you consider goals for your child, ask yourself the following questions:
- What natural talents and abilities is my child already showing? For example, some children are naturally compassionate and enjoy doing things for others; others display a keen interest in discovering how things work.
- What can I do to encourage these natural talents? Could I ask my child to draw pictures or make cookies for an elderly friend or for our new neighbor? Could I provide building materials, blocks, and small gadgets for her to construct and desconstruct?
- What areas do I need to help my child work on? For example, does he need to develop his self-help skills? Can she learn how to show empathy for others?

- What things have I noticed that help my child truly thrive? Does he need structure, extra sleep, small frequent meals, time alone, extra snuggle time? The answers will be as varied as the children.
- How can I enrich the environment so that my child gets enough of these things? Do we need to have a well-defined schedule? Should I change our meal times? Should we create a quiet space?

Lentil and Kale Soup

2 bags green or brown lentils
2 boxes chicken broth or 8 cups of homemade broth
2 cups water
2 large carrots, diced

1 onion, diced
1 bunch of kale leaves, finely chopped
1 package of gluten-free kielbasa*
Salt and pepper as desired

Combine all ingredients in a large pot and boil for 30 minutes. Turn heat to low and continue simmering for another 20 minutes. Serves eight. If you make a double batch, you can freeze half for an emergency meal. *Note: Substitute any type of sausage that your family likes.

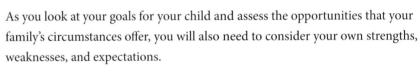

As you look at your goals for your child and assess the opportunities that your family's circumstances offer, you will also need to consider your own strengths, weaknesses, and expectations.

Realistically examine your own personality. You might have definite opinions about what a child should learn and when. There are many theories of education, and even the two authors of this book hold differing opinions on the subject: Kathy prefers an eclectic developmental approach, allowing her children to direct some of their studies toward their interests and leanings. Lesli teaches at a co-op with other homeschooling families, where even the preschoolers learn memory work in a classical school setting. Despite our different approaches, all of our children are growing and blossoming

Here are some questions to get you thinking about your own strengths, weaknesses, and expectations:
- Are you okay with letting the kids get messy, or will you need to plan the messier activities outside or away from your home?
- Do you appreciate a well-planned day, or do you prefer to wing it?
- Will it be hard for you to do open-ended activities without being concerned about the end product?
- What about my personality will make me a terrific teacher for this child? (If you are naturally self-deprecating, ask one of your most honest and encouraging friends.)

- What about my personality could potentially cause problems?
- What plans and boundaries will I put in place for myself to head off these problems before they occur?
- Is there anyone in my life (partner, friend, experienced homeschooling mom) who will hold me accountable on days when I just don't feel like following through on my homeschooling commitment?

We all have strengths and weaknesses that can affect the atmosphere of the home. It is important to honestly assess yourself and seek accountability for those areas that could prove detrimental to your child's education. For example, if you tend to be a person who struggles with consistency or spends too much time on the phone or the computer, you will need to address these issues before you begin. It could be that you agree to check your email only twice per day or that you find an accountability partner to make sure that you are actually schooling your child. If you are the type of person who loves to have a spic-and-span home, it can be very tempting to pop your child in front of a video and just clean. You may need to come up with a plan to handle these temptations in advance.

As a family, you will need to assess your priorities and circumstances. Use the opportunities provided by your circumstances to teach your child. For example, perhaps you are caring for an elderly parent. As your child sees your example and even participates in caring for this family member, he will learn patience and sacrifice and will develop a heart for serving others. There is nothing like learning history from an eyewitness, and spending time with someone who has seen a great deal of life can provide a rich learning experience for your child. Be encouraged that your unique situation, however inconvenient or unconventional, can be mined heavily for treasure to invest in a precious little person. If you approach teaching your child with a positive attitude and endeavor to enjoy learning along with her, it will be a winning situation for your entire family.

As you consider your family's priorities and circumstances, ask yourself the following questions:
- What unique opportunities can be found in our current season of life that can be used to teach our child life skills and good character?
- Are there unavoidable difficulties (financial hardship, illness, and so on) that I need to think through and mine for treasure?

A Note from Lesli

This last exercise can seem a little discouraging. Take heart. You were chosen as the parent of your child—strengths, weaknesses, and all. Acknowledging the areas where we are weak helps us build up and fortify. Your love for your child can give you resolve and impetus for change and growth like nothing else!

When I started homeschooling, I knew that I tended to be inconsistent and flighty. I love my children too much to allow those character flaws to interfere with their education. I resolved to be consistent, and I asked my husband to hold me accountable. Just acknowledging my shortcomings and resolving to address them made a huge difference in helping me to overcome these personal weaknesses.

- How can both parents be involved in this child's educational experience? Do we need to adjust schedules to allow for more involvement for the working parent?
- Are there opportunites for business travel that we can use to our benefit to educate our child?
- Are there service opportunities that we would like to take part in as a family that we can incorporate into our preschool experience?
- What values are important to our family, and how can we incorporate these into our preschool curriculum?

Not only will you be able to prepare your child for kindergarten, but also you will be able to teach him life lessons. One of the wonderful things about educating your child at home is that you can instill the unique values and characteristics that your family esteems. We have emphasized the following character traits with our families. Your list may differ.

- Understand that actions have consequences.
- Tell the truth.
- Share.
- Put others first.
- Empathize.
- Be fair; don't show favoritism.
- Be a good steward.
- Be neat.
- Don't complain.
- Work hard.
- Respect authority.
- Be thankful.

So, how will you make this all work? How will you reap the harvest? As you read, you will see that this book encompasses a lot more than just educational information. When you decide to educate your child at home, life is no longer compartmentalized. Homeschooling integrates all parts of life, and you will need to make adjustments in all areas to achieve a healthy balance. After all, the time has to come from somewhere! We have included housecleaning and organizing tips, recipes, and advice for tough times. Teaching our children at home has grown us in so many areas, and we are eager to share with you the way others have shared with us.

Chicken Enchiladas

3–4 chicken breasts or whole chicken, cooked and shredded
1 can chopped green chiles
2 cans enchilada sauce
Cheese,* shredded

16 tortillas
Black olives, pitted and sliced
Tomatoes, diced

Combine shredded chicken with green chiles and one can enchilada sauce. Fill each tortilla with a large spoonful of the chicken mixture. Roll and place filled tortillas crease-down in two 9" x 13" pans. Pour remaining can of enchilada sauce onto the enchiladas. Sprinkle with cheese. (If desired, cover with foil and freeze for later use. Thaw enchiladas in the refrigerator.) Preheat oven to 350 degrees. Bake enchiladas for 20–30 minutes. Garnish with sliced black olives and diced tomatoes. *Note: Our family likes Rice brand cheese alternative. Use any cheese that your family prefers.

Chapter 2

LEARNING THROUGH PLAY

T̶ake a few minutes to think back to your own childhood—what did you do as a child? We have asked thousands of people this question over the years, and the majority of the people say, "We played!" Childhood should be full of making memories, discovering, experiencing, and, yes, playing! Research supports the value of learning through play in early childhood. The key to understanding how play prepares children for kindergarten is to understand how children learn when they play.

Young children learn best when they experience concepts in a real way. For example, if the goal is to teach a young child about an apple, giving the child a coloring page with a picture of an apple is not the best approach. The child needs to see a real apple. She must touch the apple, even cut it open and check out the seeds and the star inside. The child must smell the apple, taste it, and hear it as it crunches.

Real experience builds a strong foundation for learning as the child grows. Once a child enters elementary school, he has the ability to build abstractly on this concrete foundation. However, if a strong foundation is not built at the preschool level, the child will suffer with developing and understanding abstract concepts.

*Tell me and I will forget.
Show me and I will remember.
Involve me and I will
understand.*

—CHINESE PROVERB

Psychologist David Elkind says it best:

> *In our hurried and hurrying society, we have come to think of play as a luxury at best and a waste of precious time at worst. From our adult perspective, we often associate play with fun and relaxation in contrast to the attention and effort required of us by work. All too often, however, we mistakenly project our grown-up conception of play onto the play of children. Yet for children in general, and for young children in particular, self-initiated play is a basic mode of learning. Through such play, children create new learning experiences that they might not otherwise encounter.*
>
> —"Learning through Play," CommunityPlaythings.com

Chipotle Chicken

2 7-ounce cans chipotle chiles in adobo sauce

½ cup olive oil

1 red onion, sliced

2 teaspoons ancho chile powder

10 garlic cloves, pressed

2 tablespoons dried oregano

Black pepper to taste

3 pounds chicken thighs or breasts

Combine first seven ingredients to create marinade. Place chicken in two ziplock freezer bags. Divide marinade between the two bags. Put in freezer for later use. Thaw in refrigerator for a day prior to use. Remove chicken from bags. Grill chicken thighs 6–8 minutes per side. Breasts take about 10 minutes per side.

Children develop socially, emotionally, physically, and cognitively. Well-rounded development requires attention to every area. Let's take a closer look at these developmental areas.

SOCIAL DEVELOPMENT

Around the age of three, your child will begin participating in cooperative play; she will seek out a friend to play together. Socially, preschoolers are less self-focused and more independent than toddlers. Most preschoolers are able to work out their own disputes; however, they will sometimes need guidance and encouragement from adults to use their words instead of using physical force. Through open-ended play, children can have opportunities to develop their social skills. As preschoolers play together, they will need to work out who gets what costume, who gets to be the princess/firefighter/doctor/superhero, or how to share the favorite blocks or toys.

As your child enters her fourth year, her social skills continue to develop. You will witness your four-year-old adding details into her role playing. For example, a three-year-old might enjoy exploring the play kitchen and play food; a four-year-old will role play as Mom, Dad, or another adult as she plays with the items. Susan Engel, a psychology professor and contributor to *The New York Times* says the following about play: "Play—from building contraptions to

enacting stories to inventing games—can allow children to satisfy their curiosity about the things that interest them in their own way. It can also help them acquire higher-order thinking skills, like generating testable hypotheses, imagining situations from someone else's perspective, and thinking of alternate solutions."

While a three-year-old is usually willing to play with any friend, a four-year-old will begin to seek out specific friendships and even refer to some as her "best friend." A four-year-old may be able to work out her own disagreements, but she will still need adult help to navigate through difficult peer situations. For example, during a disagreement, it is common to hear a four-year-old state that a child is not her friend anymore. An adult can step in and help the children identify the real root of the problem and help them discover an appropriate solution.

In *Caring for Your Baby and Young Child: Birth through Age 5,* the American Academy of Pediatrics says that inviting your child's friends into your home offers an opportunity for him to "show off" his home, family, and possessions to other children, thereby establishing a sense of self-pride. The home does not need to be luxurious or filled with expensive toys; it needs only to be warm and welcoming.

EMOTIONAL DEVELOPMENT

Three-year-olds are learning the balance between independence and boundaries. Listening to your child during fantasy play is a great way to discover valuable information about his emotional development. Many three-year-olds aren't yet comfortable expressing their emotions verbally to another child or adult but can role play a situation to show an emotion. For example, your child might be playing with baby dolls when you notice one doll begins comforting another about the monsters in the closet. Chances are, this is an issue for your child but he might not have been able to express it to you. Another telling scenario might be watching your three-year-old build with blocks and then suddenly knock them down out of anger. Upon further investigation, you discover that the tower represented the new house that you are building and that your child is fearful of leaving the only home he has ever known.

As children approach age four, they develop a better understanding of basic emotions such as happy, sad, and mad. They also begin to discern when they are feeling jealous or guilty. Yet, young children still need adults at times to help them identify their emotions. Emotional development is strengthened during open-ended play. For example, when a child has her toy taken away, it is appropriate for the preschooler to express sadness or anger. It is equally appropriate for a child to squeal with delight when she discovers that red and blue make purple. When a child is struggling to express her emotions, an adult needs to step in and support the child. You might do this by asking the child how a situation made her feel. Suppose one sibling hits another during a disagreement. First, stop the fighting and encourage the children to use their words to express what just happened. You may need to walk the children through this process by helping them identify the emotions they feel: angry, sad, frustrated, jealous, and so on. Knowing themselves emotionally is powerful for children and will serve them well into adulthood.

PHYSICAL DEVELOPMENT

The physical development of a child is more obvious than some of the other stages. Most adults show great excitement as their child moves through a physical stage. Generally, the physical development of a child is broken into two areas: gross motor development and fine motor development.

If you have ever watched a child skipping over the lines on the sidewalk or jumping like a bunny across a playground instead of running, you have seen gross motor development in action.

At the preschool stage, it is important to engage your child in a variety of activities to build his fine motor skills. It is through many play-based activities that a young child will build the fine motor skills necessary for writing For example, when a child is manipulating clay, he is strengthening the fingers that will later use scissors to cut

A Note from Lesli:

When I was an inexperienced mom with my first preschooler in tow, I can remember my exasperation as my three-year-old daughter insisted on carefully balancing on the brick edge of the sidewalk as she walked to the car every morning. It took her forever to walk that short distance! Now I know that she was practicing her gross motor skills. I wish someone had told me—I would have been more patient with her!

paper and hold a pencil to write his name. As a child is weaving ribbon through a strawberry basket, her fingers are preparing to draw letters and numbers. What children see as play, adults recognize as opportunities for building skills that last a lifetime.

Cognitive Development

By the age of five, most children know the entire alphabet, begin rhyming words, can understand the concepts of yesterday, today, and tomorrow, and have a vocabulary of more than 1,000 words. The rate at which preschool children learn new concepts is phenomenal.

Talking to a child is the best way to help her develop verbal skills. This can take place throughout the day. Use life situations as learning opportunities. Explain how the money gets to the tube at the teller window; ask your child open-ended questions about her day; and take the time point out the fascinating things in life, such as rainbows and spiderwebs. Read to your child. Encourage her to tell you about the story, characters, and illustrations. Encourage her efforts to read the story to you.

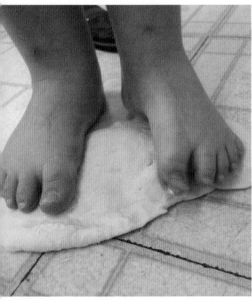

Ask your child questions that encourage him to think and reason: Why does it rain? Why can't we see the sun at night? Listen to his explanations without judgement, and then discover the answers together. Encourge your child to play with puzzles; she will not only develop her fine motor skills but also learn to problem solve.

In her well-known 2009 article in *Time* magazine entitled "The Growing Backlash against Overparenting," Nancy Gibbs includes an anecdote from Dr. Stuart Brown, a psychiatrist and the founder of the National Institute for Play. He relates that managers at Caltech's Jet Propulsion Laboratory (JPL) noticed the younger engineers lacked problem-solving skills, despite having top grades and test scores. The managers realized that the older engineers had more play experience as kids—they'd taken apart clocks, built stereos, and made models. JPL eventually incorporated questions about job applicants' play backgrounds into interviews.

Provide your child with lots of opportunities to experience childhood through discovery. For example, when you provide a child with paint in the colors blue and yellow and the child discovers green, it is a powerful learning experience. The child is much more likely to remember the concept of green because of her discovery. Many times we want to simply inform the child of the color green by pointing out the green grass or a green crayon. While this information is helpful as a support system for teaching, it should not be the primary way we teach young children. When the child experiences the mixing of two colors to create a third, his brain will create a foundation-building moment. When he sees those colors in the future, he will connect to the moment of mixing colors, and he will know green!

Allowing your child to experience activities in an open-ended manner will impart a deeper understanding at the preschool level. There is a saying that has been stated in the preschool education world for many years, "It is the process, not the product." When a young child wants to decorate his pumpkin in a unique way, ask yourself, "Why not?" Why not let the child use the colors he chooses? Why not allow him to place the eyes where he sees them? The child is simply interested in creating, and it is in the creating that true learning takes place. In creating, the child expresses himself, his uniqueness, his vision. This freedom to create will instill in the child a desire to learn, a desire to discover, a desire to take risks.

In the second section of this book, we have listed many activities for you to try with your preschooler. We chose these powerful activities to help you grow your preschooler at home. For example, when we suggest that you make playdough for your child, we know that your child will see that playdough and will jump for joy. You can smile, too, knowing that playdough is a valuable tool for learning. With this simple tool, your child can explore and develop math, language, social, science, and fine motor skills. Your child will learn math as she maneuvers the dough, figuring out how much dough it will take for the perfect elephant ears, or comparing her fat snake with her sister's skinny snake. She can use playdough to build letters and numbers in 3-D, which will help her see these symbols in a concrete way. While she plays with playdough, you may hear, "Look at my butterfly," or "I made you a cookie," thus stretching social and language skills. This open-ended activity encourages children to take risks and try new ways to create. Playdough is science; your preschooler will explore mixing ingredients to create a new substance and identifying its characteristics as smooth or rough, smelly, or grainy. Her fine motor skills are strengthened as she pounds, cuts, and manipulates the dough. If you make a large batch of dough, she will develop her gross motor skills as she squishes her toes in or jumps on the mound of dough. Playdough is a powerful learning tool.

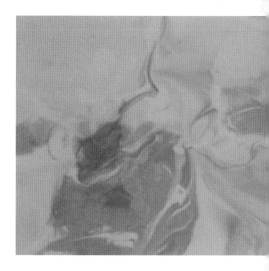

Imagination is more important than knowledge. Knowledge is limited. Imagination encircles the world.

—ALBERT EINSTEIN, physicist

A Note from Kathy

My oldest son has a great imagination! When he was a young child, I took him to a local bookstore to make Mother's Day pictures (with magnets attached to the back). The instructor provided glue and lots of collage materials. Most parents were assisting their children, helping them put the materials on the circle in a uniform fashion, making lovely magnets for their fridges.

John Michael worked alone as I watched. He was fascinated with the glue. He squirted glue in a circle, and then in lines—he used a lot of glue. Some of the parents were looking at me with that panicked look, wondering when I was going to take over and save my Mother's Day gift. I didn't.

His glue dried, and my magnet was the coolest one in the group (and he had the most fun!). That magnet hung on our refrigerator for many years and brought such a smile to my face.

Was he simply playing or was he learning? Both! He was creating what he wanted to express. He was using the glue as the decoration, not a foundationfor other decorations. He was experiencing the characteristics of glue (science). He was using his hands to hold the glue bottle and move it all over the paper (fine motor skills). He was trying to figure out how much glue it would take to fill the paper (math). He was creating (art). As his mother, I knew that day that I had a child who thought outside of the box.

Play is powerful. It is in play that future scientists are made. It is in play that great debaters have their first debates. It is through play that children often discover their passions, their personalities, and their preferences.

The best way to ensure that your child has gained a particular developmental skill is to plan activities that promote that skill set. The activities in this book will help you plan a variety of learning experiences for your preschooler. During these activities, observe your child's social interactions, fine motor skills, gross motor skills, and so on. It is not necessary to test your children by asking them to show you how they hop on one foot or walk backward. Take the time to be an intentional observer during your child's play. If you observe how your child plays and interacts with others, you will know where your preschooler is developmentally. If you notice that your child is not developing in the areas mentioned, talk with your pediatrician. Trust your gut—if you suspect that something is not right, get help. Early intervention is the key to ensuring that your child has the most successful life possible.

Gluten-Free Muffins

½ cup butter or olive oil

½ cup honey or whole cane sugar

1 egg

1 cup milk

1 teaspoon vanilla

2½ cups gluten-free baking mix (recipe follows)

1 teaspoon salt

1 teaspoon baking soda

1 teaspoon baking powder

½ cup chocolate chips, blueberries, diced apples, or
    peaches (optional)

Preheat oven to 350 degrees. Melt butter in a microwave-safe bowl. Stir in egg and honey. Add 1 cup milk and vanilla, and stir. In a separate bowl, stir together the dry ingredients. Combine wet and dry ingredients, stirring until batter is smooth. Add chocolate chips, blueberries, apples, or peaches, if desired. Place paper muffin cups in a pan, and fill each cup two-thirds full. Bake at 350 degrees for 15 minutes. Makes 12 muffins. Recipe can be doubled or tripled.

Gluten-Free Baking Mix

3 parts brown rice flour

3 parts tapioca starch

2 parts sorghum flour

1 part soy flour

Stir ingredients together, and store in an airtight container. Make a double batch to keep in the pantry for muffins, pancakes, and desserts.

Chapter 3

SOWING
THE SEEDS
PRESCHOOL
LEARNING

Now that we have taken stock of our overall goals, let's take a look at what you need to do by the time your child blows out five candles on the birthday cake! While we have chosen to homeschool our children, we understand that many families will choose to enroll their children in traditional schools for kindergarten. It is our aim to cover all of the developmental and educational bases so that your child can make a good transition from the homeschool environment to a kindergarten classroom. In the activities section, we've included lots of ideas for preparing your child for a lifetime of learning.

Pausing to listen to an airplane in the sky, stooping to watch a ladybug on a plant, sitting on a rock to watch the waves crash over the quayside—children have their own agendas and timescales. As they find out more about their world and their place in it, they work hard not to let adults hurry them. We need to hear their voices.

—CATHY NUTBROWN, educator

COMMUNICATION AND EMERGENT LITERACY SKILLS

Your child's vocabulary will grow at an enormous rate in the preschool years. Talk with your child, ask open-ended questions, and share stories. Make up simple rhymes and songs, or recite and sing favorite ones. Read together and talk about what you read. Play listening games, such as I Spy and Simon Says. The more your child communicates, the better her speaking and listening skills will be. Before your child enters kindergarten, she should be able to speak in complete sentences of more than five words, recall and relate parts of a story, and take turns listening and speaking in a conversation.

Surround your child with opportunities to connect letters with the sounds they symbolize. Provide an environment rich with words. Talk with your child about the names for things in the environment, the steps in a recipe, and the details of items you see every day. Read, read, read! As your child begins to recognize letters, encourage him by offering lots of open-ended writing opportunities. What starts out as scribbles will very soon become recognizable letters and creatively spelled words.

A Note from Kathy

When my oldest child was in kindergarten, many of his friends had started to read. As a first-time mom, it was hard not to compare John Michael to the other children. Even though my son couldn't read, he was passionate about books. I was confident that I had laid a strong foundation in literacy, and I continued to encourage him by reading to him and providing literacy and language activities. Once he began to read, he took off. I am so thankful that I didn't give in and push him before he was ready. Today, he loves to read and has a passion for words.

MATHEMATICS SKILLS

Math learning opportunities are everywhere. Describe and talk with your child about the characteristics of objects: compare shapes, sizes, colors, and patterns. Sort items by same and different, smallest to largest, shortest to tallest, and lightest to heaviest. Use positional words such as *near, far, top, bottom, under, first, second,* and *last.* Provide opportunities for your child to connect numerals with the quantities they symbolize.

Number awareness, the idea that the symbols mean something, starts to develop around three years of age. One-to-one correspondence shortly follows. By age five, a child should be able to count 10 or more items and be able to do simple computation; match a picture with an object; and have a beginning understanding of time, including the concepts of now, soon, and later. Math concepts are so easy to teach, because we use them so often in everyday life!

PHYSICAL SKILLS

Gross motor skills involve the large muscles of your child's body, which enable her to walk, kick, sit upright, lift, and throw. For these skills, your child needs both muscle tone and strength. Provide your child with plenty of opportunities to run around obstacles, throw a ball overhand, and catch a large ball overhead. Encourage her to climb a ladder, slide independently, and ride a tricycle. By age five, a child should be able to alternate feet when climbing stairs, stand on one foot for 10 seconds or longer, hop, skip, and swing. Plan trips to your local park, play outside with your child, and choose active games that will help your child develop these skills.

Fine motor skills involve using the smaller muscles of the fingers, toes, lips, and tongue in coordination with the eyes. A firm foundation in fine motor skills is essential for the skills needed later on for writing and other forms of communication. Provide opportunities for your child to copy simple shapes such as crosses, circles, triangles, and rectangles. Encourage him to draw a person with a body and to print some letters. Provide simple puzzles for him to assemble and blocks for him to use for stacking and building. Help him learn to dress himself and care for his own toilet needs, skills he should master by his fifth birthday.

Weave music throughout the day. Play an upbeat song and dance together. Practice clapping on the beat of a favorite rhyme or chant. Overlap emergent literacy and motor skills when listening for rhyming sounds in your favorite song as you tap out the beat with wooden spoons. Sing together as you play or walk outside.

A Note from Lesli:

As a preschooler, my son's autism affected his ability to share his emotions. Autism can make it difficult for a person to identify emotions before acting on them. His difficulty with communicating drove him to many tantrums and behavior problems, but he has come a long way. Recently we were at a supermarket, and he accidently knocked over a display of cans while we were at a supermarket. He was mortified, and his first impulse was to bolt from the store into the busy parking lot. I saw what was about to happen and said, "Think of a word to tell how you feel!" He said, "I, I, I—I'm abashed!" The stress and embarrassment just melted out of his body, and we picked up the cans together and moved on.

SOCIAL AND EMOTIONAL SKILLS

Talk about your feelings, so your child will develop a language for expressing emotions. Ask your child how he feels, and listen to his response. Use developmentally appropriate stories from your own life to discuss moods and manage conflicts and feelings.

Provide opportunities for your child to follow simple directions and to help with household tasks. Encourage sharing, taking turns, and asking for help when needed. Provide opportunities to make choices between two options. Help him to learn accepted rules for behavior, to notice other people's feelings, and to manage his own feelings and reactions when he does not get what he desires.

Science Skills

Preschoolers are natural scientists. They easily investigate, experiment, and discover. Provide your child with lots of opportunities to show curiosity, ask questions, and explain why things happen. Ask your child to use words that describe change, motion, position, order, and attributes such as color and size. Encourage him to use his senses to observe, describe, and predict what will happen next in his environment. Provide opportunities to compare and group objects according to characteristics such as shape, size, living or nonliving, and so on.

As you look at the activities section of this book, you will notice that the activities are grouped into developmental areas. However, it is important to note that learning is not isolated in one area at a time. When your child is painting, she is not only participating in art. She is also developing her cognitive skills as she decides what to paint, her language skills as she tells you about her painting, her sensory skills as she fingerpaints or paint with textures, her fine motor skills as she manipulates the brush or her hands, and even musical skills as she sings along to the music you are playing while she paints. If you use the activities and ideas provided in this book, your preschooler will learn what she needs to succeed in kindergarten, whether at home or in a traditional school setting.

Chapter 4

SETTING THE STAGE

When you think of growing your preschooler at home, you might think that you need to set up a preschool classroom to do it right. Not so! We recently reviewed a beautiful book that was full of pictures from several preschools. Surprisingly, most of the pictures looked like someone's home.

Many preschools are now designing their school spaces to resemble the home because the home is a natural environment for learning. This is good news to the teacher of a homegrown preschooler. Your home is the perfect place for learning to occur. Let's take a look at a typical preschool classroom.

> The most effective kind of education is that a child should play amongst lovely things.
>
> —PLATO, Greek philosopher

CIRCLE TIME AND BOOKS

During circle time in a typical preschool, children are listening to books and talking about the weather, the calendar, and daily life. Traditional preschools use circle time to teach children the importance of sitting quietly while others talk. Circle time also provides a child with his first opportunity to speak in front of a group. Can this be done at home? Absolutely! The skills of sitting still and listening attentively can be taught almost anywhere. It is not the shape that you sit in or the number of children in the group that is important. Much more significant is picking quality books, reading them with enthusiasm, and teaching children to listen with interest! The sofa, the kitchen table, and the backyard are all ideal places for reading and sharing about life with your preschooler.

Keeping baskets of quality books around your house will offer constant opportunities for reading to your preschooler. Take books with you outdoors to provide a completely different experience for young children. A colorful blanket, a porch swing, or even the trampoline can make pleasant reading spots.

> Good books provide support for the kind of character we hope to see developed in our children.
> —GLADYS HUNT,
> *Honey for a Child's Heart*

Smoothie Ice Pops

2 cups frozen fruit (strawberries, blueberries, peaches, cherries)
1 frozen banana
1 tablespoon honey (optional)
1 cup milk or orange juice
Ice-pop sticks
Ice-pop molds

Puree ingredients in a large blender or food processor. Pour into ice-pop molds, adding an ice-pop stick to each, and freeze.

In a typical preschool, circle time is the place where the discussion of life and current events occurs. The children get to tell about what's going on in their homes, about their day, their vacation, their pet dying, and so on. The teacher really listens to the children, demonstrating that their voices and perspectives are important.

You can achieve the same goal with your child. Simply listen. If given the opportunity, children will fill your ears. Children need to learn how to express themselves, their ideas, their views of their world. This can occur naturally in our homes, but with the inundation of technology, it can be difficult. Be intentional about making space to listen to your child. When you are in the car with your preschooler, turn off the DVD or the radio and talk. Ask your preschooler to share a story of his day. Discuss the weather or start a countdown for an upcoming event or holiday. At home, keep phone and computer time to a minimum. Take walks around your neighborhood. This uninterrupted time with your preschooler provides opportunities for discussions about life and the big and small issues occupying his mind. Circle time really is one of the easiest areas to transition from the preschool classroom to the home.

BLOCKS

Block play in the typical preschool classroom consists of colorful blocks in a variety of shapes, trucks and cars, and usually a train set or two. This space is usually combined with the circle-time space, because the children use a large area for building. This is usually a popular area in the classroom and quickly fills up during center time or free play. Block play is very important to the preschool child's development. It provides the opportunity for learning concepts such as spatial awareness and balance. The block area is also great for social and cognitive development because children are working together, discussing the best options for building their roads and towers.

Include explorations with blocks in your homegrown preschool. You can buy a good set from a school supply store. Alternatively, you can make your own at home: Fill block-shaped boxes with shredded paper, and tape them closed.

Cover the boxes with contact paper or duct tape. Large Duplos and Legos are also great additions to your block area. If you have space, designate a place for blocks. A low shelf is ideal, but a large container is sufficient. Keep the blocks near a flat space so that the child can have room to build when she desires. For a change of pace, take your container of blocks outside where your child will be encouraged to try new types of construction. The uneven surfaces and textures outside can provide more challenges for building and balance than the kitchen floor offers.

HOUSEKEEPING AND DRAMATIC PLAY

The housekeeping and dramatic play area is a favorite center in most preschool classrooms. Pretend play offers so many learning opportunities, and preschool-age children find great pleasure in pretending. Pretend play is a must for the homegrown preschooler. Let's consider housekeeping first. What is the housekeeping area anyway? This is the place where children typically pretend to be the adults in their lives. They cook like Mommy or Daddy or pretend to make the foods they eat in their favorite restaurants. They set the table, take orders, and prepare a favorite meal.

There are two ways to approach this housekeeping concept in the home. You can supply a child-size kitchen set for quality play opportunities. You can find one at most toy stores, educational supply stores, or your local thrift store or a garage sale. Filling the kitchen area with empty boxes and containers from your kitchen is a natural way to merge home and play. Most preschool teachers provide a homelike environment in the preschool classroom. This should excite the teacher of a homegrown preschooler; you already have the home environment, and you have the real kitchen, too.

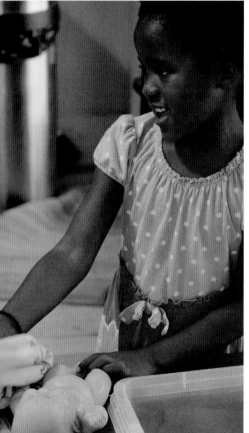

While pretend play is important, do not neglect the real kitchen! Quality learning takes place there: measuring flour and water, smelling vanilla and peppermint, squeezing lemons for fresh lemonade. The learning that can happen and the memories that can be made in the kitchen are endless. For example, your child can help make all of the recipes in this book. Kitchen activities provide great opportunities for developing math skills (measuring), science (chemistry of combining ingredients), language (naming ingredients and learning vocabulary), social skills (taking turns pouring), and fine motor skills (dumping, sifting, stirring).

What is more fun than dressing up? The typical preschool classroom is full of dresses, ties, purses, necklaces, and costumes. Children enjoy being the cowboy, fireman, and princess. Offer your homegrown preschooler the same experiences. In the typical classroom, the dress-up clothes are kept in a container. At home, you will need to decide where to keep all of these dress-up items. You have a couple of options. If you have room in your home, you can hang hooks along a wall at the child's level. If you are handy, you can build a dress-up cabinet. Or, you can simply use a large plastic container. The key is to provide a variety of dress-up items for your child. Note: Your child will request to wear her princess costume or cowboy boots and hat to the store at some point. And, why not? Dress-up and pretend play can happen anywhere.

MATH AND MANIPULATIVES

In a preschool setting, math and manipulative areas usually include a storage shelf and a table. On the shelf you will find puzzles, lacing cards, Legos, counting bears, pattern blocks, and math games. At the preschool level, the focus of math is quantitative concepts, number awareness and recognition, one-to-one correspondence, measurement, shapes, sequencing and patterns, and simple computation. We offer a number of math activities, such as Shoe Measuring, Count Your Own Snack, and Placemat Puzzle, that address these concepts.

The beautiful thing about growing your preschooler in a home environment is that math is everywhere in the home. Sorting socks is a math experience (one-to-one correspondence). So are putting toothpaste on a toothbrush (comparing the quantities of *a little* and *a lot*) and finding the rectangles in your house (shapes). Of course, you can buy math counters and pattern blocks at a school supply store; just make sure you don't overlook the math in your everyday life. Count how many steps to the mailbox, measure ingredients for dinner, and subtract each chicken nugget your child eats. This is math!

The purpose of a manipulative area in a preschool classroom is to build fine motor skills and teach mathematics in a hands-on way. This is why you see small things in a manipulative area, such as puzzles, lacing cards, beads, and small building materials. These items encourage young children to use their fingers to manipulate, gather, and sort. In a classroom, manipulatives are usually rotated on a regular basis. We suggest you have enough manipulatives in your arsenal for a two- or three-week rotation. One week the choice might be tweezers and pompoms, two puzzles, and linking people. Another week the choice might be lacing cards, connector blocks, and keys and locks. This area can easily be implemented in the home. You can create a manipulatives bin and rotate the items with your preschooler. In the fine motor section, we have listed many examples for these types of activities; and in Chapter 7, we have storage suggestions that will help you to easily rotate them.

Language and Emergent Literacy

Writing centers in a preschool classroom consist of a small table and chairs, baskets of pencils, paper, and some tracing materials. This center is used to encourage the preschooler to hold a pencil correctly and to begin forming letters and shapes. Often there are sentence strips with the students' names and some basic sight words on them. Getting a child comfortable with the pencil and the concept of writing is the goal of the preschool teacher.

In the home, make pencils, paper, and words readily available. Give your children opportunities to "write" throughout the day. They might decide to "write" a letter to grandma or create a shopping list for you. (Our children love little hand-sized notebooks to carry around!) When you see your child desiring to do these things, it shows that your preschooler is valuing the written language and is on the wonderful road to becoming a reader and a writer!

Another way to help a child value words is to provide a journal for writing and storytelling. Composition notebooks are wonderful for this and go on sale before school starts every year. Stock up! As often as possible, encourage your preschooler to draw a picture in his journal, a picture that tells a story. After he has completed his drawing, ask him to tell you about his picture. Write down what he says, word for word. This is not the time to correct grammar or content. This is your child's story, how his preschool mind views the world. It will give you great insight if you take the time to listen. As time goes by, you will be amazed at how the stories change and develop. Those journals will become treasures as the years pass.

Homemade Granola

6 cups rolled oats, regular or gluten-free
12 tablespoons butter
¾ cup honey
coconut, sliced almonds, sunflower seeds (as desired)

Preheat oven to 400 degrees. In a saucepan, bring honey and butter to boil for about a minute. Remove from heat. In a separate bowl, stir together oats and other desired ingredients. Spread oat mixture evenly into a 12" x 15" jellyroll pan. Pour honey butter over oat mixture. Bake for 10 minutes. Stir, and bake for another 5 minutes. Store in an airtight container.

Preschool-age children develop their language skills at a rapid rate. The best way to build your child's language development is to engage in regular conversations with him and read to him on a daily basis. Ask your child open-ended questions to encourage him to use the language he has learned: "Tell me about your picture," or "What was your favorite thing that happened today?" or "How should we decide who gets to go first in this game?" As your child's vocabulary grows, you can ask him to tell you a story instead of simply answering a question.

One of our favorite language activities is making books. Provide your child with some magazines, paper, crayons, and glue. She can make books about so many topics, from *My Favorites* to *Animals That Fly* to *Things That Are Blue.* Let your child tell you the words to write to caption her pictures. Children love to look at their own books, and they can usually "read" them cover to cover.

Many people ask us about the alphabet. Is it necessary to have the alphabet posted in the home? No, it's not necessary. However, if you want the alphabet in your home, go for it. There are wonderful, aesthetically pleasing alphabet posters and cards on the market that blend in with home decor. Regardless, we suggest that you display written words around your home. Having a print-rich environment is beneficial for preschool-age children. Labeling things with sentence strips is a concrete way to help children connect words with items. For example, seeing the word *door* on the door helps the child make a connection between the two. Very few isolated letters have meaning; let your child see the letters organized together into words.

A special teacher, Mrs. Diana Risher, gave me my first journal when I was a student in her classroom. I still journal today, writing about my thoughts, dreams, prayers, and fears. Journals provide young children a place to do the same. Help your child start a journal at a young age. Your child might be intimidated at first, but he will quickly get the hang of it.

In the beginning you might need to encourage your child with starters such as the following:

- I wish…
- Tomorrow, I will…
- Yesterday, I…
- I am scared of…
- I really like to…

Or, you can simply ask your child if she has a story to tell. Write down word for word what your child says (no correcting allowed). Encourage your child to illustrate her story. This is a great memory-making idea as well as a great learning tool for young children. Often, the child will use storytelling as a way to express her feelings about a certain situation she is dealing with. The following story was written by Addie, a special four-year-old.

My aunt, not my aunt, she died in Heaven. I love her. I love her in my heart. I am glad that she is in Heaven. I love her in my special heart.

COMPUTERS AND
OTHER ELECTRONIC DEVICES

We are the pioneer generation in using technology to assist in the education of our preschoolers. The perks and pitfalls are only now being researched and reported. Use common sense, have a healthy and cautious awareness of what is out there, and keep abreast of new technology as it arises. We have been surprised several times when our children have stumbled upon things we'd rather they not see, so we want to start this off with a warning: Supervise children as they use computers and other devices that connect them to the Internet, just as you would supervise them when they are outside your home.

Technology will no doubt be a big part of your child's life and will become second nature to him as he grows. Teach your child to see technology as an interactive tool. As you use technology throughout the day, point out its uses to your preschooler. Talk about how the ATM works, and let him slide the card. Explain the difference between a landline phone and a cell phone, and have your child memorize both numbers, so that he can reach you in an emergency. Purchase a cheap or used digital camera for your child to use to explore photography—add the photos to his journal! There are many children's storybooks available for electronic tablets; they are kind of like a modern version of the pop-up books that we enjoyed as children.

The National Association for the Education of Young Children (NAEYC) and the Fred Rogers Center for Early Learning and Children's Media issued a policy statement in March 2012 that affirms that the use of technology tools in intentional and developmentally appropriate ways, and in conjunction with other traditional tools and materials, can support the development and learning of young children. This position statement is available online at the NAEYC website, www.naeyc.org.

The American Academy of Pediatrics (AAP) advises that children under the age of two have no screen time at all, and that children older than two should have no more than one or two hours of screen time per day. Numerous studies suggest that excessive screen time contributes to attention-deficit disorder, behavioral issues, obesity, and sleeping problems. Even if you choose to use electronic tools with your child, the majority of her day should be spent in child-directed, open-ended play; messy art and sensory activities; and outdoor fun. There are some great educational apps available when you need them, but we strongly suggest limiting screen time for a preschooler.

SENSORY PLAY AND SCIENCE

The sensory area is an exciting center in most preschool classrooms because it is completely process oriented. Typically, you will see a sensory table with a variety of elements inside. One day you might see sand, another day you may see cornstarch and water, and on still another day, dry beans or rice. This is one of the easiest areas to create at home.

You can buy a premade sensory table from a school supply store, or you can make your own from materials found at your local hardware store. (We have included instructions for a simple sensory table in the Appendix on page 195). If you don't have the resources or space for a sensory table, you can easily use a large plastic container, round tub, or a large aluminum foil pan. The children will enjoy the excitement of sensory play regardless of the container.

Sensory play is of incredible value to the preschool child. Provide your preschooler with many opportunities to experience and discover; sensory play creates scientists! When your child is mixing colors, ask her to guess what will happen (create a hypothesis). Invite her to actually mix the colors (test the hypothesis). Observe and discuss the results with your child.

Some adults are wary of sensory play because of the potential mess. One of our favorite sayings is "Being a kid is dirty, messy, noisy work." Sensory exploration might be a little messy, but the educational benefits make it worth the mess. If you are truly concerned about the mess, set up your sensory play outside.

Many other science activities occur in a preschool classroom outside the sensory table. For example, you might find magnifying glasses, bird books and binoculars, rocks, cocoons, and even a pet or two in the science area. Many of these items can easily be added to your home.

Learning to look deeply at things is the heart of science. Modeling this to a young child will pique his natural curiosity and set him on a path to lifelong learning. How does science exploration look in the homegrown preschool? Take time to notice interesting things. Ask your preschooler to consider how something works. Encourage your preschooler to be aware of her surroundings. Stop and smell the roses, literally. Pick up a bird book and a pair of binoculars, and identify the birds that live in your yard. Invest in some magnifying glasses and use them to examine objects and creatures in the environment. Explore the properties of magnets. Take nature walks. Purchase a sketch book for your preschooler (and one for you) and create nature journals together. Draw pictures of the world around you, and discuss those pictures. Invite your preschooler to tell you stories about her pictures, and write those stories down. Find a place in your home to create a nature center, and display in it some of the beautiful things that you find: a bird's nest, a special pinecone or rock, a turtle shell, and so on. Enjoy exploring science with your preschooler.

ART

String art, marble art, and plunger art—any way you look at it, art plays a vast role in the life of a preschooler. The art center in a preschool is usually filled with items such as crayons, paper, stickers, scissors, glue, chalk, magazines, torn paper, and paint. Easels are often available for preschoolers to use to further express themselves artistically. You may be wary of setting your preschooler loose with paint in your home. Take a deep breath—you can do this. Art is powerful for young children. It allows them to create the world as they see it. Following is a list of materials to get you started on gathering items for your child's art explorations. Don't be afraid to try out your own or your child's ideas! Art can be created from almost anything:

- Collage materials
- Glue
- Scissors
- Stickers
- Paper of various sizes and textures

- Magazines
- Paint of various types: tempera, fingerpaints, water colors
- Brushes of various sizes
- Sponges

We have included many age-appropriate art activities for your preschooler in this book. These activities will provide lots of opportunities for your preschooler to express himself and grow his brain at the same time. If you cannot get past the thought of making a mess inside your home, take your art to the garage or outside. The garage is a great place for an art center; it won't take up a lot of space and the location makes cleanup a breeze.

Exploring art expands a child's ability to interact with the world around her and provides a new set of skills for self-expression and communication. Not only does art help to develop the right side of the brain, it also cultivates important skills that benefit a child's development. But art goes far beyond the tangible statistics measured by studies—it can become a pivotal mode of uninhibited self-expression and amazement for a child. Art matters the same way language matters! Art is a fundamental component of what makes us uniquely human.

—MARYANN KOHL,
artist, teacher, and writer

The Great Outdoors

The woods were my Ritalin. Nature calmed me, focused me, and yet excited my senses.

—RICHARD LOUV,
Last Child in the Woods:
Saving Our Children from
Nature-Deficit Disorder

In today's average preschool, the outdoor areas consist of climbing equipment, a slide, sand or mulch, and maybe some swings. Providing a quality outdoor experience for your child will be an easy task—the world is your playground! Let's look at how to use the great outdoors to benefit your child's development. Don't let the indoor duties of life keep you or your preschooler from enjoying being outside. Nature is beautiful! Grab your preschoolers and get out in it. Nature is a great teacher. Take a blanket, some books, and maybe a snack. Read to your preschooler outside. Lie down and find shapes in the clouds, tell stories to each other about the shapes you see. On a cool fall morning, bundle up and head out to explore the colors, sounds, and smells of a new season. Climb trees, and jump on rocks. Admire a beautiful sunset. Take a hike or go fishing at a friend's pond.

Take lots of pictures to document your time outside. This will provide you and your child with memories for years to come. We have a friend who keeps a basket of nature and wildlife guides, magnifying glasses, bug boxes, and binoculars by the back door. Use wildlife and plant guides to learn about the organisms you see, and teach your children to name creatures and plants by their proper names.

Play outdoor games and activities: playing hopscotch, bouncing balls, and riding trikes all contribute to the gross motor development of a preschooler. Moving the easel outdoors provides many new landscapes to give your artist inspiration. Provide a bucket of water and a large paintbrush, and let your child "paint" the driveway, the house, rocks, and anything else he can find! Your scientist will enjoy mixing sand and water on the patio. Even your young waiter will enjoy taking your order on the porch "restaurant." Simply moving an indoor activity outdoors can completely change the experience for a child.

If your budget allows, climbing structures, swings, and slides are great additions to your outdoor space. If you are handy, you can make your own seesaw and balance beam. Plan regular playdates at your local park to ensure that your child is getting time to run, jump, and climb. Without large pieces of equipment, children can still develop those large muscles by jumping rope, Hula-Hooping, skipping, and playing chase games in their own backyard.

In the Appendix we have provided a Getting Started Checklist on page 189 to help you prepare your home for learning.

Sweet and Crunchy Chicken

6 pounds boneless, skinless chicken breasts

2 cups honey

1 cup spicy brown mustard

¾ cup olive oil

1 tablespoon salt

1 tablespoon granulated garlic

1 tablespoon black pepper

3 cups panko or tortilla crumbs

1½ cups pecans or almonds, finely ground

Cut chicken into strips. Mix honey, mustard, oil, salt, garlic, and pepper in a medium bowl. In another bowl, mix the panko or tortilla crumbs and ground nuts. Dip each chicken strip into sauce, then into the crumbs until completely coated. Place chicken on greased cookie sheet. If desired, freeze until solid, and then store in freezer bags.

Serving day: Preheat oven to 350 degrees. Place strips on cookie sheet, and bake for 30 minutes or until chicken pulls apart easily and is no longer pink in the center.

Chapter 5

HOME LIFE = LEARNING

SLOW DOWN AND TEACH

One of the marks of our society is the constant push to do everything in the fastest, most efficient way possible. We find ourselves rushing from one activity to the next, constantly struggling to keep up. Unfortunately, in the home, this often leads to feeling like we don't have the time to let little hands help with the everyday tasks. After all, even the best of us struggle with how to get it all done, and sometimes it just feels more efficient to do a job yourself.

As home educators, we must shift our thinking in several ways. There is a lesson in everything; we just need to be willing to slow down and teach it. This attitude is freeing in so many ways and comes as an unexpected surprise to many parents or caregivers who endeavor to grow preschoolers at home.

Take a deep breath, and slow down.

Creative people are curious, flexible, persistent, and independent with a tremendous spirit of adventure and a love of play.

—HENRI MATISSE, artist

Think with us for a moment about the first things you do when you wake up. You hear the stirrings of your little one, and you stumble downstairs to make some coffee. Think about the steps you go through: measuring water, pouring, scooping, counting—in the very first activity of the day are rich learning opportunities. Imagine the joy on your child's face as you allow him to share in your morning ritual, to pull a chair up to the counter, to do important adult work! Together, you can listen to the sound of the water rushing out of the faucet into the carafe, your faces pressed together as you check to see if the water is level with the appropriate line. Little hands nest the filter into the machine, and you count scoops of fragrant coffee as you dump them into the basket. Your happy child pushes the button and listens for the satisfactory "drip, drip" to begin. Together you wipe up water that has missed the mark, and any errant coffee grounds. It is 6:15 a.m. and in a very small gesture of cooperation, you have poured much into your child.

It sounds like a simple thing, but it really is a radical mental shift for many people. After years of educating our children at home, we have come to realize that the learning experiences that we have with our children in these everyday minutes are so rich. Shift your mindset and start seeing the opportunities that are right in front of you on a daily basis. Capture these moments of pure joy and connection as your children learn in your home.

Tropical Slow-Cooker Ribs

10 pounds baby back ribs
1 tablespoon soy sauce or tamari
3 cups catsup
1 tablespoon lemon juice

3 cups water
¾ cup pineapple juice
1 tablespoon chopped garlic
½ cup brown sugar

Brown spareribs in medium skillet or under the broiler (watch carefully!). Divide between two freezer bags. Combine remaining ingredients in saucepan. Bring to a boil on the stove. Reduce heat, and simmer for 10 minutes. After sauce has cooled, pour half the sauce over the ribs in each bag. Remove as much air as possible from the bag and seal it.

Serving day instructions: Thaw completely. Place meat and sauce in slow cooker, and cook on low for 7–8 hours. To bake in oven instead, place meat and sauce in a large baking dish, and bake at 350 degrees for 1½–2 hours.

COOKING, SORTING, SCRUBBING—OH MY!

There are certain things that have to happen in our homes every day for us to function as healthy families. One of the worries of taking on education at home is whether or not we will be able to meet all of our obligations while teaching our kids. In reality, involving kids at an early age in the upkeep and maintenance of the home is beneficial for everyone! Think about the developmental and emotional skills that children can gain as they take part in these activities.

FOLDING LAUNDRY

Laundry can be a wonderful learning opportunity for a young child. A three-year-old can easily fold a washcloth, learning to match the corners, folding it in half, then folding it in half again. This simple activity involves eye-hand coordination, fine motor skills, and eventually, fractions, as we say, "Fold it in half. Now into quarters." Gradually, as the child is ready, this folding activity will translate to clothes. There, the idea of symmetry begins to form. The child is learning the beginnings of geometry and fractions, enjoying a feeling of being close to you, and participating in important work!

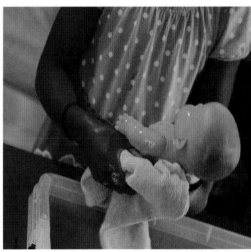

Here are some other ideas for including your preschooler in the laundry process:

- Let him dump hampers out and bring you the laundry in a wagon.
- Teach her to sort lights and darks.
- Teach him to match socks.
- Encourage her to name colors of items as you sort.
- Encourage him to name the family member an item belongs to.
- Let her climb a step stool to help load the washer (with your help).
- Let him deliver the freshly folded clothes to the owner in a small basket or wagon.

The degree to which preschoolers love helping with laundry is amazing. They are quite accurate in matching clothes to family members, which indicates that they are paying attention to what is going on in their home. Their enthusiasm is contagious and improves an adult's attitude about this sometimes dull and burdensome chore as well.

KITCHEN HELPER

The kitchen is a fascinating place for most children and is a sensory playground for the developing brain. Think about this for a minute as we focus on each sense. Their eyes take in the varied colors of fruits and vegetables. They learn about hard and soft as we search for the ripest pear. The kitchen may be the first place they learn about hot and cold. Pleasing aromas abound. They learn about smooth and crunchy and have access to a variety of textures to feel. It would be difficult for even the very best preschool to rival your kitchen for sensory stimulation!

You must always have safety in mind when working with children in a kitchen, especially when using step stools. Move any potentially dangerous items to an out-of-reach location, and do not let your child get close to the oven or stove. Please do not ever leave your preschooler unsupervised!

Baked Tilapia with Mango Salsa

1 cup plus 2 tablespoons all-purpose flour

1 cup plus 2 tablespoons cornmeal

1 tablespoon garlic powder

3 tablespoons dried parsley

3 tablespoons dried basil

1 tablespoon kosher salt

1½ teaspoons black pepper

1½ cups beaten egg

1½ cups buttermilk (or milk with 1 tablespoon lemon juice or vinegar added)

18 four-ounce tilapia fillets

Olive oil

1½ cups grated parmesan cheese

1 jar mango salsa

In a large, shallow bowl, combine the flour, cornmeal, garlic powder, parsley, basil, salt, and pepper. Mix thoroughly, and set aside. In a separate shallow bowl, combine the egg and the buttermilk. Dip the fish in the egg mixture, and then dredge in the flour mixture until completely covered. Place the breaded fillets onto three greased baking pans. Sprinkle with olive oil and parmesan. Cover with plastic wrap, then with foil. Freeze for up to three months.

Serving day instructions: Thaw breaded fish. Preheat oven to 450 degrees. Bake, uncovered, for 8–10 minutes until the fish is crisp and golden brown. Serve with rice and mango salsa!

Here are some hints for teaching your child in the kitchen:

- Consider placing dishes on a low shelf so that your preschooler can help set the table.
- Let your child help unload the dishwasher. Just make sure that you unload anything sharp or fragile before giving your child access to the dishwasher.
- Allow your child to fill drink glasses from a small pitcher or from the faucet.
- Let your child help with washing fruits and vegetables, and let her taste them as you work.
- Invite your child to help you measure ingredients.
- Encourage your child to put away canned goods on low pantry shelves. Great stacking and matching opportunities abound!
- Let your child help in safe ways with baking and cooking: stirring, adding ingredients, pouring, and so on.

You may have to demonstrate a task several times before your child wants to try. Continue modeling the behavior or task while talking through the steps: "We put the cup into the soapy water, and then we scrub it with our brush. We rinse it with nice clean water. Now we put it here to dry. Where does the cup like to hide? In the cupboard!"

Edible Fingerpaint

Color vanilla Greek yogurt or pudding with food coloring, and let your preschooler paint with her snack!

Most children love to cook and bake. Be mindful of talking through the steps whenever you are measuring ingredients. Food is a great math manipulative, and it is pleasing to the senses. Allow your preschooler to play with measuring cups and dry rice, beans, or water. A younger child will enjoy just pouring, while an older child may investigate how many quarter cups fit into one cup. Place a folded beach towel on the floor under a bucket filled with water, and allow your child to dip a measuring cup and pour water back into the bucket to his heart's content. (Just make sure to clean up quickly when he is finished, to avoid any damage to your floor.) Consider purchasing child-safe tools for the kitchen. Many are available online or at retail kitchen supply outlets. We have included a list of some of these retailers in the Appendix.

Cooking and baking offer important science learning opportunities. For example, you can easily demonstrate forms of matter (chemistry) using water: make ice, let the ice melt into its liquid form, and then boil water to show your child steam. Talk through the reasons for adding different ingredients as you cook: for example, "The eggs will make our cake fluffy," or "Honey will feed our yeast so it will bubble up and give our bread the energy it needs to grow tall."

As you work and explore together in the kitchen, teach your child the importance of a balanced diet. Consider purchasing a felt board from a school supply store, along with a set of nutrition felt shapes. Mount the board on the inside of your pantry or lower cupboard door. Let your preschooler help choose foods that make up a healthy meal. For an older preschooler, practice reading labels. Read serving sizes out loud, and help the child measure or count the appropriate amount. Learning portion control is an important step in building healthy eating habits for adulthood.

Don't be afraid of a mess. Keep some beach towels around to spread under your child, and consider purchasing a sheet of clear plastic from your local fabric store. You can lay the plastic over any tablecloth or tabletop to protect surfaces without compromising your home decor. Many fabrics can be laminated as well.

CLEANING

Most young children love to clean. It makes them feel productive and helps build a healthy attitude about work. Being aware of the mess one makes on a daily basis is an exercise in noticing detail and living conscientiously without burdening others or the environment—a lesson best learned early. Helping to clean up demonstrates consideration, kindness, and good stewardship and is one of the earliest building blocks of self-care.

Start at your child's level. Dusting baseboards is a good chore for little ones. Shadow your child through the day, and verbally and physically model the steps for cleaning up. If your preschooler has a stubborn streak and doesn't want to clean up after herself, gently and firmly move her hands to pick up the toy and put it where it goes. In a cheerful tone, say, "Now the toy is put away! Well done," and move on.

Here's a list of chores you can encourage your child to help with:

- Dusting baseboards
- Wiping spindles of staircase rails
- Picking up toys and games
- Wiping and straightening lower cabinets in bathrooms and kitchens
- Wiping low windows
- Washing dishes
- Picking up and sorting items
- Vacuuming with a small, handheld vacuum

In our homes, we have some small laundry baskets with laminated photos of family members glued onto them. This makes it easy for a toddler to pick up items in a room and put them in the right basket.

Washing dishes is a good activity after breakfast and lunch. Consider placing a plastic baby pool on the floor and setting two tubs filled with warm water inside. Put some dish soap in one of the tubs, give your child a dishrag or scrub brush, and let him wash some dishes while you work next to him at the kitchen sink. This activity can stretch out, because young children never seem to be done with soapy water!

Note

Provide children with safe and natural cleaning supplies. White vinegar is one of our favorites. A little vinegar in a spray bottle can clean just about anything. The smell almost immediately dissipates, and you can add some favorite essential oils to it—we love lemon and orange. There are many websites and books dedicated to making your own healthy cleaning supplies.

Keep your little one's age and ability in mind as you encourage her to help around the house. Chances are that she will not complete a task with anything near the neatness or efficiency that an older child or adult would bring. If she washes a window, you may have to go behind her later and clean it again. (Just don't let her see you doing this.) The goal is to help your child feel important and helpful, confident and positive, and valued as a member of the family. Attitudes, both good and bad, are contagious, so be mindful of your voice and tone as you work. Encourage your child and thank her for being a great helper.

Chapter 6

WHO HAS TIME FOR THIS?

There are so many types of families in the world. For every family, there is a different schedule. As you create a schedule that incorporates homeschooling, consider your family's priorities. Stick to a routine that honors and reflects those priorities and values. As you transform your home into a school as well as the place where you live, you will need to balance the roles of teacher and parent appropriately. Let's look at what needs to take place in each of these spheres.

All labor that uplifts humanity has dignity and importance and should be undertaken with painstaking excellence.

—MARTIN LUTHER KING, JR.

ADDRESS YOUR OWN NEEDS

Take good care of yourself. Failure to do this can lead to resentment and burnout.

Tend to your personal nurturing and growth as a parent and teacher by regularly devoting time to the following areas:

- Spiritual growth and reflection
- Exercise or other physical activity
- Nutritious and balanced meals
- Personal relationships with other adults
- Time for planning and preparation
- Personal business (i.e., checking email, paying bills, running your home business, and so on)

We suggest altering your schedule so that you get up earlier than your preschooler does. It is very helpful to get some part of your self-care routine out of the way before your child wakes up. For Lesli, that means taking a shower and getting dressed, making her bed, and tidying her room. For Kathy, it means getting to the gym for a workout before her kids wake up. You may find that you want to use those moments of quiet in a completely different way, such as having some time alone with your mate or enjoying a cup of hot tea and reading. Having this time alone in the morning can put you ahead of the game when your preschooler wakes.

Meatball Stew

3 medium potatoes, peeled and diced

3 celery ribs, chopped

1 large onion, chopped

1 pound fresh baby carrots

1 14-ounce package frozen meatballs

1 can condensed tomato soup

1 can beef gravy

1 cup water

1 envelope onion soup mix

2 teaspoons beef bouillon

Place vegetables and meatballs in a five-quart slow cooker. In a bowl, combine the remaining ingredients and pour over meatball mixture. Cover and cook on low for 9–10 hours or until vegetables are done. Note: If you make this in a big turkey roaster, you can do a quadruple batch.

A Note from Kathy and Lesli

When my children were little, I belonged to an organization called Mothers of Preschoolers (MOPS), which gave me great support and helped me to recognize that I would be a better mom when my own needs were met. In their wonderful book called *What Every Mom Needs*, Elisa Morgan and Carol Kuykendall address how to find the balance between meeting the needs of your family and meeting your own needs. Fill your own tank to ensure that you have the mental and physical energy to enthusiastically educate your child.

You can also find time for those other important personal activities during nap times or when your child is wrapped up in an activity that you can supervise while taking care of some of your own business. You can read a book while sitting in the backyard letting your child play with sidewalk chalk or blocks. You can bring out the fingerpaints and pay some bills while your child paints. Break your necessary tasks into the little chunks of time you have available.

ADDRESS YOUR CHILD'S DEVELOPMENT

On a weekly basis, a home educator of a preschool-age child needs to provide that child a balanced diet of activities in the following areas:

- Home life
- Science
- Gross motor
- Fine motor
- Math
- Language and emergent literacy
- Art
- Social-emotional

There are many factors that determine when and how you would work these activities into your day. We will address a variety of possible scenarios.

Ashley and her husband, Kevin, have one daughter. Ashley is a stay-at-home mom who has chosen to teach her daughter at home through the preschool years. An ideal day for Ashley might look something like this:

Ashley sets the alarm to wake up an hour before her three-year-old gets up. Then she dresses, tidies her room, works out, and spends time in spiritual reflection. When Rosalie awakes, Ashley is ready for the day.

Ashley sings good-morning songs to Rosalie as she dresses her. She helps her place her pajamas in the hamper and pull her blankets up neatly on the bed. As they go down the stairs, they count them together. Ashley has planned a menu for the week that includes pancakes for breakfast. Together, they gather the ingredients, and Ashley pulls up a chair for Rosalie to stand on. They measure and count as they mix the batter. When the griddle is hot, Rosalie watches from a safe distance as Ashley counts the circles of batter on the pan. Ashley seats Rosalie at the table and gives her a small plastic pitcher of juice with a small amount of juice inside. She allows Rosalie to pour her own juice into a sturdy cup. Rosalie is very pleased at this and pours the juice back and forth between the pitcher and cup while the pancakes cook. Together, they eat breakfast.

Ashley points to the calendar located near the table, and says that this day, Monday, is the day they visit Grandma. Ashley asks, "Is it raining? Should we take an umbrella?" Rosalie looks outside and sees the rain dripping on the windows; she nods her head. This will be exciting! Together they rinse their dishes and tidy up the kitchen. Rosalie is able to place the baking powder back on the low pantry shelf.

They sit on the couch with a basket of books fresh from the library. Rosalie likes to hear one particular book over and over, and Ashley obliges, even though the repetition gets a bit tiresome. They decide to go outside with umbrellas to investigate the puddles. They find earthworms and listen for frogs, deciding to hop like frogs all the way home. Back inside, they make a picture of their walk to give to Grandma. Ashley helps draw, and Rosalie traces over her mom's lines with a crayon. Rosalie adds lots of raindrops and other details. Ashley can't tell what they are, but she asks Rosalie to tell her about the picture.

Soon it is time for the visit to Grandma's. During the drive, they listen to a folk-music CD for children with songs about rain. Rosalie claps and wiggles in her seat. She loves music! When they arrive at Grandma's, Ashley reminds Rosalie of the rules: We don't run in Grandma's house, and we are allowed to touch her coffee-table breakables with only one finger. Rosalie enjoys giving Grandma the picture she created and looking at Grandma's special items. Ashley appreciates that Grandma is teaching Rosalie how to behave around fragile items, rather than just putting the items away.

They have lunch with Grandma. After thank-yous and hugs goodbye, they return home. It's time for Rosalie's nap. They read *Goodnight Moon* and *So Many Bunnies,* and they sing "Hush Little Baby." Rosalie is used to the routine and goes to sleep without a fuss most of the time.

During nap time, Ashley returns calls and emails and does a few housekeeping chores. She defrosts something for dinner and decides how to spend the rest of the afternoon with Rosalie. She realizes that in the morning she was able to provide Rosalie with gross motor activities (jumping in puddles), fine motor activities (pouring juice and coloring), math activities (counting stairs and measuring for pancakes), music (recorded music in the car and singing at home), and language and literacy activities (reading, talking about the weather and nature outside). She notices that Rosalie has not had an opportunity to play with building materials or to experience sensory play. She also wants to work on teaching Rosalie to set the table before Dad gets home.

Ashley sets up an area for Rosalie to play with blocks, so that it will be ready for her when she wakes. After nap time, Ashley finishes paying the bills while Rosalie plays. Later, they set the table together and go outside to pick flowers. Ashley finds a flower in the botany book and tells Rosalie that it is a hydrangea. Inside, Rosalie makes flowers out of playdough while Ashley cooks dinner. As she cooks, Ashley looks at her chart on the refrigerator and sees that she has met her daughters developmental needs for the day.

Of course, this is an ideal day. We left out the spilled juice, the tantrums from both mom and child, and the playdough up the nose. But we have given you a snapshot of how you can accomplish teaching during a normal day at home. Days differ, and you may have visitors, lessons, and playdates, but this does not change your ability to give your child a varied diet of developmentally appropriate activities. Often, outside lessons cover one or more of the areas on your chart, and a playdate provides the perfect opportunity for your child to develop social and language skills. Pull out some of your best activities when your child has a friend over; it is a great time to learn about taking turns and sharing.

"Help!" you cry. "I have three children ages four and under! How can I make this work without pulling my hair out?" Take heart, and read on!

Shredded Chicken with Barbecue Sauce

6 chicken breasts
1 large onion
Garlic powder to taste
Bottle of your favorite barbecue sauce

This is one of the easiest recipes for a busy family. Place chicken breasts in a large slow cooker. Add whole onion on top. Sprinkle garlic powder on the chicken breasts. Cook for 4–6 hours on low. Shred the chicken, and add barbecue sauce. Serve on buns or as a stand-alone main dish. If desired, freeze some of the shredded chicken before adding barbecue sauce, and use it for another recipe later.

David and his wife, Mandy, work in the medical industry, sharing the responsibility of caring for and teaching their three young boys. On this day, David is in charge of Luke, age four; Jackson, age two and a half; and Sam, age eight months.

An ideal day in David's life might look like this:

David wakes an hour before the boys and gets in a run on the treadmill. His wife leaves for work before the children wake. David prepares a pot of oatmeal and a warm bottle for the youngest son. Sam is the first to wake up, and he is hungry. David feeds Sam while singing his favorite morning song, "Twinkle, Twinkle, Little Star." Jackson and Luke wake and are also ready to eat. Luke helps Dad by getting bowls and spoons from a low shelf while Dad finishes giving Sam a bottle. Jackson gets napkins for everyone and sits down with a smile. David puts the baby in the high chair with a few Cheerios and serves the oatmeal to the older boys.

During breakfast, David tells the boys about the big day they have planned. It is Tuesday, the day they meet up with a few other dads and their kids at the park. Luke sees the sun peeking through the curtains and comments on the pretty day ahead. After breakfast, Luke and Jackson help clear the table. Luke helps put the dishes in the dishwasher. David takes all of the boys back to their room and gets them dressed for the day. Mandy had made some sensory bottles for Sam, and David gives them to him to explore while David reads some books to Luke and Jackson. Luke wants to take a turn "reading" *Brown Bear, Brown Bear, What Do You See?* and Jackson is impressed with his big brother.

During Sam's morning nap, David has some fun activities planned for the two older boys. They love sensory activities, so David pours some cornstarch and water into a large plastic bin, creating a blob that oozes delightfully when you pick it up. The results are fabulous! The boys mix and play and play and mix. When the fun is over, the boys help David sort and match socks. While the boys are matching socks, David decides to start working on dinner prep.

Later, David has some time to help the boys make entries in their nature journals before Sam wakes. David grabs his binoculars and the bird book and heads outside. The yard is full of cardinals, finches, and eastern phoebes. The boys draw their favorite birds in their journals and tell their father something about their drawings. He writes their thoughts down word for word. Sam wakes, and it is time for snack: apples and rice cakes. David and the boys then head to the park with scooters and trikes for a playdate with friends.

David wants to make sure the boys get in some music before the day is over, so back at home, David turns on the soundtrack for *Beethoven Lives Upstairs* and pulls out the bin of Lincoln Logs for Luke and Jackson. David sits on the floor with Sam, rolling a ball back and forth. Jackson decides the ball is more interesting than the logs and takes over. Later, during Sam and Jackson's short afternoon nap, David reflects on the activities Luke has enjoyed. He feels that some more age-appropriate book time would be beneficial and reads *St. George and the Dragon* to Luke. Luke wants to paint a picture of a dragon for his mom, and since the two little boys are napping, David allows Luke to use the watercolors to create his masterpiece. While Luke is happily painting, David finishes dinner so the family can eat together when his wife arrives. After dinner, David collapses.

In this scenario, we deleted the two blow-out diapers, the panicked call from the office, the Lego in the toilet, and the mother-in-law who dropped by during what will forever be known as the Cornstarch Incident.

"That's all well and good," you think, "but what about my family? The Duggars make it look easy, so I thought I could do it. How do I handle educating my many, many children?" First bit of advice: The Duggars are lovely people, but quit comparing yourself to them! Real life doesn't come with an editing department. But, it is possible to homeschool children and teens of a variety of ages.

Rebecca and John Michael have six children, ages two, four, six, nine, twelve, and fourteen. Rebecca is a classical educator who has found that homeschooling the older four comes naturally, but having both a preschooler and high school student brings challenges she did not anticipate.

Her teenager likes to stay up late and talk, while her baby likes to get up early. This makes it hard for Rebecca to maintain her routine of waking one hour before her baby. When she fails to do this, she feels like she starts the day already behind schedule. Her teenagers participate in sports and have practices in the afternoons, which makes it difficult to catch up on housework or rest while the baby is sleeping. Rebecca feels like she is spending her life just catching balls as they are thrown at her. How can she give her preschooler a quality experience when there is so much competing for her attention? Let's look at how an ideal day might look for Rebecca:

Rebecca sets her alarm for 6:00 a.m. and gets up to shower and do her Bible study before her kids wake up. She knows that she needs to stay on track for the day to start out right. At 7:00 a.m., she wakes the children, beginning with the oldest child. Rebecca knows that there is no physical way for one person to do everything that needs to be done for a family of eight, so she starts the children on their morning to-do lists. Everyone is expected to pull his weight from an early age.

She puts on some classical music to set a peaceful tone in the house. The four older children dress and tidy up their rooms. The kids take their laundry to the laundry room, and fourteen-year-old Lauren starts the first load of the day. Twelve-year-old Noel unloads the dishwasher, and nine-year-old Joshua helps six-year-old Isabelle set the breakfast table.

Rebecca consults her menu plan and sees that it's Monday, which means muffins and smoothies for breakfast. Thankful that she has had a few cook-and-freeze sessions recently, she pulls out some frozen batter for muffins. As the muffins bake, the older kids take orders for smoothies.

Once everyone is fed, Rebecca goes over the memory work for the week. This week they are memorizing skip counting by twos, the parts of speech, the names of the continents, Latin declensions, and timeline cards. Although the two- and four-year-old don't understand the concept behind skip counting (multiplication), they do enjoy the rhythmic chanting of the others and try to join in. The younger children also like looking at the pictures on the timeline cards.

After this, the most difficult task is math, so Rebecca starts this next. All the children except Lauren work at the table together so that Rebecca can answer questions. Lauren, the oldest, does her math in her room using a teaching CD that can work through any problem that she has trouble with. Rebecca gives the two-year-old and four-year-old animal counters that they sort into muffin tins; little Phoebe follows her older sister Piper's every move. Rebecca helps Isabelle, Joshua, and Noel with their lessons. While they are working, Phoebe and Piper decide to move to playing blocks on the floor. Rebecca watches the math students carefully, and corrects their errors on the spot, so that they do not cement incorrect thinking into their studies.

When math is over, Lauren takes the little ones to the basement to play with musical instruments while Rebecca works on language and literacy with the older kids. Lauren can use a 20-minute break from her studies, so this is fine with her! Rebecca works with Isabelle and Joshua on phonics and reading. When the music stops, Joshua takes the little kids outside to play on the trampoline, which gives them a chance to practice gross motor skills. Lauren has some questions about her writing assignment for British literature, so Rebecca helps her with that while she watches the kids on the trampoline. Rebecca then takes Noel aside and quizzes him on his timeline cards; she also asks to see the maps he has been working on. Satisfied with Noel's progress, Rebecca turns her attention to Joshua. She reads to him from *Red Sails to Capri*. The little ones have found the sand table outside on the porch and are happily pouring and scooping while Rebecca reads. Lauren drifts upstairs to finish her *Beowulf* paper.

Shortly before lunch, everyone breaks to do chores. The laundry goes into the dryer and the dishwasher is loaded. Pets are fed, and clothes are put away. It is Noel's turn to make lunch, so he boils some noodles and adds leftover grilled chicken and parmesan cheese to the pasta. Since it is a nice day, everyone decides to eat outside on a blanket with paper plates.

After lunch, the little ones go down for a nap. Rebecca uses this time to circle back with Lauren, Noel, and Joshua to see if they ran into any trouble on their writing assignments. Then, Rebecca decides to take a 20-minute catnap while they keep working. This helps her to keep up with the late nights and the early mornings! All too soon, it is time for the afternoon driving to begin. Rebecca packs the diaper bag and some snacks and gets everyone into the car to drive to ballet lessons. On the way, they listen to Jim Weiss read history on a *The Story of the World* CD.

The little ones have a chance to swing on the swings and play on the slide while the older ones have their lessons. Rebecca is able to leave Lauren at the ballet studio for her father to pick up on his way home from work. When Rebecca gets home, she realizes that, while her little ones have had lots of gross motor time while roughhousing with the big kids on the trampoline, what they really need now is some time to snuggle and read with her.

This is a night when she is thankful to pull out a casserole from the freezer and make a quick salad, because it gives her time to sit on the couch with two little ones who are a little tired and overstimulated by now. She gathers their blankets and bears, and they make a nest on the couch. She chooses some of their favorite, most comforting books, and they settle in. When Dad comes home, he is happy to join in. Rebecca slips out and finishes preparing the dinner.

Now, note that Rebecca does have to be more on her game. There is no denying that she has more balls to keep in the air than our other examples. Making a meal plan, bulk cooking ahead, and pairing her children together will go far to help her achieve her goals for educating her children, keeping her house, and maintaining her personal growth.

For those who wonder how children in such a big family can possibly get enough attention, let me assure you that the relationship our older kids have with our younger ones is one of pure joy and devotion. Our younger kids get more attention and teaching than our older ones ever did, because they have more teachers! All of our younger children have ended up academically farther ahead than the older ones were at their age, because they have spent so much time listening in as the older ones do their work. Our older children have benefited from the younger kids as they are able to review things that they have already mastered while acting as teacher. This is a classical learning community at its best.

Note from Lesli

Participating in a homeschooling co-op has made learning more efficient in our family of many ages and stages. Elementary-age children complete weekly memory work and recite daily math facts, history sentences, Latin declensions, science laws, and grammar rules. It always amazes me how much my preschoolers pick up and mimic during our memory work. It seems as though their brains are little sponges, made to memorize, in contrast to my adult brain that has to struggle. While we do not require the little ones to memorize, they do it naturally. I love the idea that when the time comes for them to learn the concepts, they will already know the basic facts!

We understand that there are days and seasons that can make it difficult to follow through with a routine. Sickness, pregnancy or adoption, and job changes may necessitate that you adapt your family schedule. In Chapter 8, we will address these issues in more detail.

As you work out the best routine for your family, imagine a day in the life of the preschooler in your home. What kinds of activities does he enjoy? In what ways can you meet the developmental needs of your preschooler with the activities that come naturally to you? What kinds of things will you need to add to ensure he has a well-rounded education? What are you excited about trying with him that you have not done before? Jot down your thoughts about the ideal schedule.

Rebecca's Chicken Pesto Ravioli

6 pounds frozen cheese-filled ravioli

1 cup chopped green onions or red onion

3 pounds chicken breasts, cooked and chopped

1½ cups pesto sauce

2 cups chicken broth

1½ teaspoons kosher salt

1½ teaspoons black pepper

6 cups zucchini, cut into half-inch rounds

1½ cups chopped tomato or red bell pepper

3 cups grated parmesan cheese

Combine all ingredients in a large bowl. Divide among three large freezer bags or three 9" x 13" pans. If desired, wrap in plastic wrap, cover with foil, and freeze for later use.

Serving day instructions: Preheat oven to 350 degrees. Thaw filled freezer bag in refrigerator. Pour contents into casserole dish. Cover with foil and bake for 1 hour until hot and bubbly. Note: If mixture is frozen in a casserole dish, you do not have to thaw before baking.

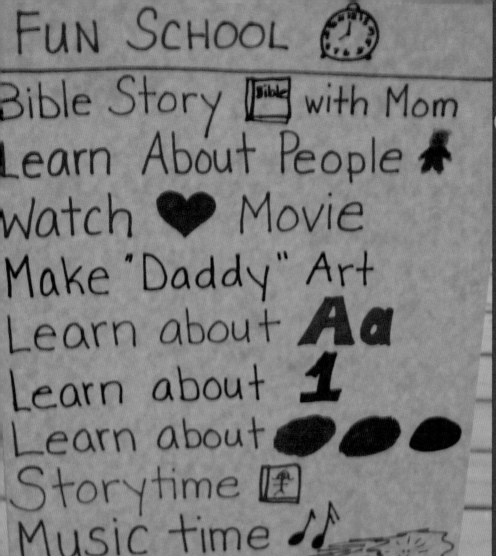

FUN SCHOOL 🕐

Bible Story 📖 with Mom
Learn About People ♟
Watch ♥ Movie
Make "Daddy" Art
Learn about **Aa**
Learn about **1**
Learn about ⬤⬤⬤
Storytime 📖
Music time ♪♫

For some of you, this chapter will rev you up. For others, the thought of organizing all of these supplies and activities is enough to make you Google the preschools in your area. Don't worry! This chapter will be just what you need to get your homegrown preschool running smoothly.

LOW IS THE WAY TO GO

Here is a job for you: Get on your hands and knees and crawl around your house. What do you see? What items can you reach? What is intriguing to you at this level? You have just experienced your house from your preschooler's point of view. When setting up an area or activity for your preschooler, low is the way to go.

Start in your kitchen. Move items around so that your child has access to his own cups, plates, utensils, and napkins. If possible, move the family plates and

Have nothing in your houses that you do not know to be useful, or believe to be beautiful.

—WILLIAM MORRIS, *The Beauty of Life*

cups to the child's level so that he can help with dishes. If you have babies and toddlers in the home, you might want to stick with nonbreakable items for now. In the pantry, you can rearrange things so that your child can reach the snack basket, spices, and other food items as appropriate. We recommend keeping a spray bottle of vinegar-and-water solution and a cloth at the child's level as well; this encourages your young child to participate in cleaning.

Yummo Honey Curry Chicken

¾ cup butter
½ cup yellow mustard
1½ cups honey
1 tablespoon curry powder
2 teaspoons salt
6–7 pounds boneless, skinless chicken thighs

Melt butter in a saucepan, and stir in next four ingredients until smooth. Rinse and divide chicken evenly among three large freezer bags. Divide sauce and pour over chicken. Seal bags and freeze.

Serving day instructions: Thaw chicken in refrigerator. Preheat oven to 350 degrees. Place chicken in an ungreased baking dish, meaty sides down. Bake for one hour or until the sauce has browned and is thick and sticky. Serve with rice.

In the rest of the house, choose bookshelves and toy shelves that are at the child's level. Look for these items at a garage sale, thrift store, or discount online site. A bit of spray paint can make these items look new. Take advantage of the wall space in your home. Mirrors are a joy for toddlers and preschoolers. A magnetic board or chalkboard hung at the child's eye level can provide hours of enjoyment for your little ones.

If you are blessed with carpentry skills, check out www.Ana-White.com. This site is full of ideas for building age-appropriate items for your home: kitchen sets, mailboxes, dress-up organizers, and more. In the Appendix of this book, we have provided the necessary plans to build your own Plexiglas easel and a light and sensory table.

Do not feel compelled to create a schoolroom unless the idea really appeals to you and you have the space! You can organize developmental areas throughout your home. One room could have the kitchen/dress-up area; another room might have a cozy corner for books and a small table for math and manipulatives. You might place a sensory and art area in your garage. The goal is to offer children a variety of spaces in which to play and discover. Take the time to think about your space, drawing it out if necessary. Think, for example, about the best place for musical instruments. It is probably not near the baby's room. Think about the best place for your art area. This is preferably an area without carpet, so that it is easy to clean up.

Check out the Getting Started Checklist in the Appendix, and make sure you have included the items you need. Do not stress if you can't immediately offer everything. Start with the basics, and build on those. Create a space for books

from pillows and blankets you have on hand. Cut the legs off an old coffee table, and use that as a surface for drawing, manipulatives, and sensory explorations. (You can use a vinyl tablecloth to protect the table and a tub for the sensory materials.) We find that when money is tight we are the most creative, so do not despair if you live in a small space or cannot purchase the latest and greatest in child development toys! A big house and lots of stuff are just not necessary for your child to get a quality education.

CONTAINER THERAPY

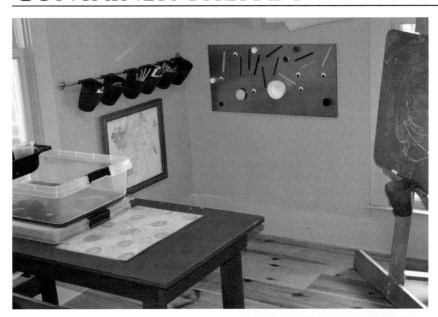

We love a good container! Having the right storage for your school supplies makes all the difference when it comes to organizing everything. Check out these pictures of some of our favorite storage solutions.

What do these pictures tell us? Be creative! Use empty paint cans on hooks to store art supplies. Low baskets are great for Lincoln Logs, books, small construction blocks, and such. A clothesline and clothespins hung at the child's eye level is great for displaying art. You could also use household molding and metal clips. Clear containers with lids come in all shapes and sizes and can store items such as puzzles, playdough, and math games. We really love wide-mouth, tall cylinders with lids. These are great for storing pompoms, seashells, pinecones, and more. Disposable plastic containers are now sold in all shapes and sizes. The smallest ones are perfect for storing paper clips, clothespins, sequins, buttons, and other small treasures. Plastic hanging shoe organizers offer ideal behind-the-door storage for items such as small papers and writing tools or for magnets or chalk.

Think out of the box when searching for containers. Try the gardening or hardware section of the home improvement store. Plastic planters, galvanized buckets, and tool organizers are pleasing places to store school supplies and toys. Rain gutters and crown molding bits make attractive mounted book and art displays. Restaurant-supply stores also have a terrific assortment of clear and rubber bins and dishwasher-safe storage containers.

Novelty Bins

There will be times when you need to make an important phone call or work with another child and your preschooler will refuse to play blocks or will have finished the activity you had planned for her. That's when you go to the closest and pull out your secret weapon: a novelty bin. Keep these plastic shoe boxes out of reach, and use them only when a scheduling emergency arises. Because of the novelty, your child will be excited when you pull them out. You can also use them as a reward system, but always pick them up promptly and put them back into mom's closet to maintain their novel status.

Top Ten Novelty Bin Ideas

1. **Floam:** Floam is an inexpensive art manipulative made of tiny, colored Styrofoam beads that can be sculpted and molded. Buy several colors and store them in baggies. Floam is neat and clean, and—because it is saved for special occasions—commands great attention!

2. **Sinky Floaties:** Put corks, poker chips, coins, paper clips, plastic animals, toy boats, and bottle caps into a mesh bag (a lingerie bag works well), and store in the novelty bin. A small aquarium net is also fun for scooping items out of water. Take the bag of items out of the bin, and fill the bin with water. Encourage your preschooler to test the items in the bag, discovering which items sink and which items float. Don't be surprised if your preschooler wanders around the house grabbing items to sink or float. If you do not want to go through the trouble of putting this together yourself, sink-and-float item bags are available commercially.

3. **Moon Sand:** Moon Sand has a wax coating on each grain, making it moldable and a little less messy than regular sand, meaning you can play with it in the house. Moon Sand is the brand name of the commercially available sand, but you can make your own using play sand, cornstarch, and water (just type "DIY Moon Sand" into a search engine). Keep the sand in an activity bin or on a sensory table, along with some of your child's favorite small toys, such as dinosaurs, cars, or farm animals. Add plastic cups and spoons for sandcastles, measuring, and scooping.

4. **Stickers:** Keep a variety of small stickers in this bin, along with a stack of small paper plates. When your child plays with stickers, encourage her to completely fill a paper plate with the stickers. You can even have her cover front and back if you are on a long phone call.

A Note from Kathy

One morning as we were working on math lessons, my phone rang. My friend had an emergency and needed me to watch her three kids in 30 minutes—for the rest of the day. When her children arrived, I was unprepared. I didn't have activities or food planned, and I was in the middle of a lesson with my older children. I pulled out the bin of playdough and put it on the kitchen counter. It kept the little ones busy so I could get back to math. Later, I took the bucket of sand containing some shovels and scoops and added that to the back porch. Voila! Kids happy and math lesson complete! Luckily, the trip to the farmer's market earlier in the week paid off: I had plenty of fruit and veggies cut and ready to serve with turkey roll-ups.

5. **Thank-You Card Box:** Create a thank-you card box with special items inside such as stickers, markers, colored pencils, and ink stamps. This is a great box to pull out after a special event when thank-you cards are needed. Write the words *Thank You* and the child's name on sentence strip for easy copying. (Note: Do not include postage stamps in your box. Your child will not differentiate them from stickers—an expensive mistake. Ask us how we know.)

6. **Mini Mixing:** Mini mixing trays, watercolors, and pipettes will keep your preschooler busy for quite some time. You can find these trays and pipettes at science supply stores and some craft stores. (See the resources list in the Appendix.) This activity can even be taken into the bathtub.

7. **Blocks on a Blanket in a Bucket:** Fill the middle of a baby blanket with building blocks. Allow your preschooler to play with them, encouraging him to use the blanket as a boundary for the blocks. When block play is over, fold the blanket over the blocks, and place them back in the bucket. Nothing is better than easy cleanup!

8. **Make It Again and Again Puppets:** Purchase a set of blank, cotton puppets, or make simple puppets by stitching together muslin cut out in desired shapes. Add some washable markers, and let your preschooler create her unique puppet family, action characters, mythological gods and goddesses, or whatever she thinks of. Throw the puppets in the wash with a stain remover such as OxiClean®, and they will be good as new for the next time you need them.

9. **Interlocking Building Set:** There are a number of great building sets on the market. (One we really like is Zoob.) Pull out a building set when your preschooler is tired of everything else. This will keep him engaged as he creates and constructs. We even laminated the pictures on the cardboard box the set came in and placed the pictures in the novelty bin to give our children some extra inspiration.

10. **Gears Building Set:** This is a great fine motor activity that is packed with variety. The interconnecting pieces move and interact, letting your preschooler create all sorts of inventions. There are several types on the market, and buying a set of these is well worth the investment!

Baggies Are for More than Food

There are blogs, websites, and e-books dedicated to the "baggie." The simple plastic, resealable bag that was created to store one's leftovers has greatly surpassed everyone's expectations. We suggest you invest in a few boxes of these impressive items. Small, large, and extra-large prove to be very handy storage solutions.

Most preschool puzzles are thick and contain a base; these puzzles fit nicely in an extra-large baggie. Cut the top off of the puzzle box, and tape the picture with packing tape to the front of the baggie. We stack ours upright in baskets, making them easy to flip through.

We also use baggies to store board-game pieces, stapling a big baggie to the back of the board. All the pieces go inside the baggie, and all the games now fit into one large basket in the cupboard. No more bulky boxes! Baggies can be used to store cards, beans, math games and manipulatives, coins, pipe cleaners, ice-pop sticks, and more.

Turkey Taco Pie

4 pounds ground turkey
4 large onions, chopped
4 cloves garlic, minced
3 cups salsa
4 teaspoons ground cumin
2 teaspoons salt
4 large tomatoes, chopped (or 3 cans diced tomatoes)

4 large zucchini, diced
1⅓ cup ripe olives, sliced
1 can of corn, drained
2 cups shredded cheddar cheese
½ cup cornstarch
1 package refrigerated pie crusts
½ cup shredded cheese

Brown turkey with onion and garlic in a large skillet. Stir in salsa, cumin, and salt. Simmer for 5 minutes. Remove from heat and stir in tomato, zucchini, olives, corn, 1½ cups cheese, and cornstarch. Freeze in four 1-gallon bags. This makes enough filling for four pies.

Serving day instructions: Thaw a bag of filling in refrigerator. Preheat oven to 400 degrees. Sprinkle ½cup cheese on pie crust, and then spoon turkey mixture over cheese. Top with another pie crust, and cut slits so steam can escape. Bake for 35 minutes. Let stand for five minutes before serving.

Large freezer bags are perfect for packing developmental activities for times that you are on the go. There are whole websites and blogs devoted to the "activity bag" in the preschool world! Do a search, and make yourself a stash of activities that will appeal to your child. These are perfect when you need things to keep your preschooler busy in a restaurant or doctor's office, when life and school need to happen at the same time.

TOP TEN BAGGIE ON-THE-GO IDEAS

1. **Sensory to Go:** Add shaving cream and food coloring to a baggie. Tape the bag closed with clear packing tape. This is a great sensory activity without the mess.
2. **Mr. Potato Head:** Any variety of this popular toy is a great activity on the go.
3. **Pipe Cleaners and Beads:** Your preschooler can string beads on pipe cleaners, creating all sorts of bracelets, creatures, or anything else he can dream up. This is a great activity for a long car ride or that dreaded trip to the DMV.
4. **Magnets:** Preschoolers love to use magnets. Provide a variety of items in the bag with some magnets, and let the child discover what sticks
5. **Dot Markers:** Place a set of washable dot or bingo markers in the bag with a stack of 5" x 8" notecards (cards work better than paper because they are thicker and sturdier).
6. **Buttons by Two:** Provide 30 buttons in a large baggie. Include smaller baggies that are labeled with the following numerals: 2, 4, 6, 8, and 10. Have the children put the correct number of buttons in each bag.

7. **Dough on the Go:** Purchase small, party-size containers of playdough (or make your own and store in snack-size baggies). Add a clean foam meat tray, small rolling pin, and plastic cookie cutters. This is a must for parents on the go!

8. **Lacing Activity:** Add yarn or sturdy string, lacing cards, and beads into a baggie. This is easy and mess free.

9. **Books:** Choose a variety, and switch them out often.

10. **Sidewalk Chalk:** This is perfect if you are on the go anywhere concrete can be found! Add a spray bottle of water, and your preschooler can clean up her art when it is time to leave.

A Note from Kathy

When we were in the process of adopting our son Joshua, we took many trips to Guatemala to visit him in the orphanage. During these visits I would pack gifts for him in baggies because they were easy to pack in my luggage. Joshua would keep his treasures in his baggies and tuck them inside his pillowcase to protect them from the hands of other boys. When Joshua came home, he had a bedroom and plenty of storage for his things. One day I was in his closet and noticed a baggie on his top shelf. It contained Legos and other special items Joshua had received since being home. A baggie means more than storage for Joshua; it represents a sacred place for special treasures.

OUTSIDE STORAGE

We have found that the trick to offering quality activities outside is to have them readily accessible. We suggest the following for outdoor storage:

- Use galvanized tins from a home-supply store to keep items such as jump ropes, water guns, shovels, sidewalk chalk, and small balls handy. Keep the tins on a storage shelf in the garage or covered patio.
- An old computer cabinet or TV armoire works great for outside storage. Paint the doors with chalkboard paint. Shelves can be organized according to use; for example, a pail of paintbrushes, containers of paint, paper, and other outside art supplies can be stored on one shelf. Bubble-solution supplies and bubble wands, along with other sensory materials can be stored on another shelf. Nature journals and colored pencils can be safely kept in a plastic container with a lid on the top shelf.
- Hang Hula Hoops, tricycles, and scooters on a low Peg-Board in the garage.
- Dump trucks, balls, and other sand and water toys can be stored in a plastic container (with holes drilled in the bottom for water to escape) or in a tall galvanized trash can with a lid (label the can to keep garbage out).

There is no shortage of beautiful and creative storage ideas on the many blogs and websites out there! Spend some time searching, and you will be sure to find some ideas for your unique space.

Chapter 8

DAYS AND SEASONS THAT DON'T FIT IN THE BOX

In Chapter 5, we give several scenarios, with the disclaimer that they represent ideal days. Many days, in our experience, don't fall into this category. Children and life can be unpredictable. What do you do on days that just seem to unravel before your eyes?

When this happens, we may be tempted to throw in the towel and give up!

PLANNING FOR *THOSE* DAYS

Be wise and plan for rough days, because they will inevitably come! Perhaps you are already in the thick of some difficult days right now, and we will talk about that. But if you have the ability, make a contingency plan just in case.

First, know what your educational priorities are. In times of illness and stress, a preschooler needs to be close to you, to feel connected. Focus on the three Rs: reading, writing, and 'rithmetic. Reading aloud to her is a great way to reassure your preschooler while still meeting her educational needs.

The time to read is any time: no apparatus, no appointment of time and place, is necessary. It is the only art which can be practiced at any hour of the day or night, whenever the time and inclination comes, that is your time for reading; in joy or sorrow, health or illness.

—HOLBROOK JACKSON, journalist and publisher

89

Second, know what your home priorities are. You may need to adjust your housekeeping standards temporarily. Think about what things are really important to you. For Lesli, it's dishes and laundry. For Kathy, it's dishes and the family room. Everyone who lives in our homes knows the minimum standard for rough days.

Third, plan for the basic physical needs of your family. For us, it comes down to having something to eat. Having a ready stash of meals in the freezer has saved us more than once on those tough days.

Baked Beef Chimichangas

6 pounds chuck or bottom round roast
1 tablespoon taco seasoning
1½ cups taco sauce
1½ cups sour cream
1 bottle or can beer (or 1 cup beef broth)
½ cup apple cider vinegar
6 cloves garlic, crushed
2 tablespoons ground cumin

2 tablespoons oregano
1½ cup canned green chilies, chopped
28 flour tortillas
1 cup butter, melted
shredded cheese
shredded lettuce
chopped tomatoes
sour cream

Rub roast with taco seasoning. Place in crock pot and cook on low for 8–10 hours. Drain off liquid and shred meat with two forks. Add next seven ingredients and mix well. On cookie sheet lined with waxed paper, form logs about 4 inches long, 1½ inches wide, and ½ inch high. Pat them into rectangles. Freeze until hard. Place them in groups of six in quart-size freezer bags, and store in freezer until ready to use.

Serving day instructions: Preheat oven to 450 degrees. Fill each tortilla with a frozen or thawed beef filling log. Roll each tortilla up, and place it seam-side down on a cookie sheet. Brush with melted butter. Bake until crispy, about 15–20 minutes. Serve with cheese, lettuce, tomatoes, avocado, and sour cream.

SLOW DOWN

The pace of life has significantly increased since we were children. There are so many great opportunities around that we want to say yes to everything. Overscheduling can get worse the older your children become and the more children you have. Sometimes, even a family that has a generally laid-back schedule can find themselves in a particularly busy season. A preschooler can feel overwhelmed by being on the go and may make his displeasure known by misbehaving and throwing tantrums.

One thing we emphasize to new homeschooling moms is the importance of saying no. There are so many fabulous field trips, lessons, co-ops, clubs, and activities. They all sound so good! Be realistic about what your family can handle, especially if you still have napping babies. If you have gotten in over your head, consider what activities you can drop. Try to schedule a couple of days in the week that you don't have to go anywhere, so that everyone has time to breathe.

If you haven't time to respond to a tug at your pants leg, your schedule is too crowded.

—ROBERT BRAULT

If you know that you can't escape the busy day, try to get a bigger bang for your buck. Choose activities that serve more than one developmental purpose. For example, on busy days, you can choose a language activity that fills a sensory need, such as writing letters in shaving cream. Play big band music as your child rides his trike on the driveway. Two-for-one activities are terrific for days like this!

Prepare for a busy day the night before. Get your backpack or diaper bag, along with lots of snacks and extra activities, ready to go by the door. Lay out clothes and shoes (especially shoes—we can never find them in our houses!). That way, getting out of the house will be easier and less stressful. Decide what the family will be eating for dinner, and take the meal out to defrost. Meal planning goes a long way to keep your food budget under control and your family healthier, especially during those busy times when you might be tempted to grab something less healthy on the go!

Take an inventory of what really needs to be done and prioritize. Get the most critical and difficult tasks done first. Then, if things have to get knocked off the list, they are the items of least importance.

Prepare a bin of educational items to keep in the car. If you are stuck waiting for a doctor's appointment or for an older child to finish a music lesson, you can make the best of your time. These should be items that your child does not get to use on a daily basis. It will feel special to get to play with them, and your child might not notice that your busy day has you feeling a little frazzled. Some of the baggie activities in Chapter 7 are easy to transport and are perfect for days like this. Audiobooks are plentiful at most libraries and are easy to download on your MP3 player.

The busy times are learning moments. Your child is watching you to see how you handle stress and pressure. You are modeling how to prioritize and organize life. This lesson is just as important as anything in a school book!

Consider the Age and the Stage

If you feel that your preschooler has entered a particularly difficult time, consider what may be going on with him. Sometimes children can be downright uncooperative. Sometimes they are just being ornery, but more often something physical or developmental is behind the behavior.

I'm Too Tired, Mom!

Has your child been getting enough shut-eye? According to the American Academy of Pediatrics, young children need between 12 and 14 hours of sleep per day. A pediatrician we know once said, "Show me a misbehaving child, and I'll show you a child who is not getting enough sleep!"

To get back on track, develop a good bedtime routine that you and your child can look forward to. Wind down with a nice warm bath. For some children, a little lavender or peppermint in their bath can be very soothing. A massage with baby lotion is calming as well. Repetition is great at bedtime. *Goodnight Moon* has been read in our home just about every night for the past 16 years!

Consider installing a dimmer switch on your child's bedroom light. This will help with the transition to bedtime. Add a blackout curtain or shade to your child's window if the long summer days are making it hard for her to settle in. Make sure that your child is comfortably and appropriately dressed. We have one child who runs hotter than the others and will wake up crying and sweaty if we dress her too warmly. Another of our children runs cooler and wears winter pajamas all year round.

If your child is still waking in the night, make sure he is getting enough to eat during the day. An active child may be just too busy exploring to eat much during the day. If you think hunger is the problem, consider offering a large snack before bed.

Even if your child will not take a nap, try to have a quiet time every day for all of your children. Your preschooler will be more cooperative if he feels like he isn't missing anything fun while he is asleep. Consider using a white noise machine if your child is particularly sensitive to noise and wakes from naps too easily.

MOM, I DON'T FEEL GOOD!

Sometimes young children don't have the verbal skills to tell us that they just don't feel well or that they are about to come down with something. Sometimes the shower of vomit says it all. Either way, unexpected sickness can derail the best-laid plans.

Be prepared! Make sure you have appropriate items on hand. Consider preparing a sick bucket for just such an occasion. Fill it with a thermometer, fever-reducing medication, homeopathic remedies, and clean washcloths for mopping foreheads.

If you have sick ones in the house, drop your expectations. Think of the day as a gift to slow down a bit. Read a lot. Snuggle. School can wait. When your kids are older, you can be mean like we are and make them do school even when they are sick. Right now, baby those babies!

MOM, I HAVE TO GO POTTY!

If you have children in a range of ages, you may have to deal with potty training a younger child while you are homeschooling your preschooler. Between the two of us we have 12 children, and we are happy to tell you that only one of our kids is still wearing diapers (and she is two years old). We are much more relaxed about this than we used to be! We have found that when kids are ready, potty training happens easily.

Still, it can be frustrating to be interrupted by constant runs to the potty, false alarms, and accidental messes while you are schooling your preschooler. Again, be flexible. We suggest putting off potty training until summer, if possible. It's easier to train children if they can run around in fewer clothes and be more aware of their bodies. They spend more time outside, so if an accident happens, it's less likely to be an issue.

If you're homeschooling, it is easy to be so focused on the lessons that you get sidetracked and forget to take your toddler to the potty. Lesli's solution was to use a clock that made bird calls every hour on the hour to remind her to take her child to the potty. It worked wonderfully, but years later when the bird calls, the kids still flock to the bathroom, kind of like Pavlov's dog.

There was never a child so lovely but his mother was glad to get him to sleep.

—RALPH WALDO EMERSON,
poet and essayist

A Note from Lesli

It may sound crazy, but I have fond memories of the pretty pink trash can my grandmother had at her house for throwing up. Have a special receptacle reserved for just such a purpose. (Our kids will probably fight over the "throw-up bowl" when we die.) Traditions are made in the strangest of places!

Our kids also love the "sick blanket," a brightly colored comforter that was mine when I was a child. The sick blanket gets spread over the couch or bed to protect the furniture from germs and other undesirable things. Just bringing it out makes our kids feel loved and pampered and helps them feel better. Often, there is nothing you actually can do to make them feel better but just ride it out, so this perception is helpful!

MOM, I'M NOT DONE YET!

Your timing might not exactly line up with your child's when it is time to switch to another activity. Transitions can lead to tantrums and behavior issues in a preschool child. Consider that your preschooler may in fact need more time, and give it to her if possible. One of the wonderful things about homeschooling is being able to see an activity to its natural end, rather than having to switch activities at the sound of a bell. If it is not going to disrupt the day completely, let your child finish a task. Be more a creature of order than a creature of the clock. If you do have to stop your child when she is involved in an activity, give her a warning at 15 minutes and at five minutes before time to stop. This will make the transition less abrupt for the child.

If transitions are difficult for the child, acknowledge improvement as it occurs by saying something like, "I know it is so hard for you to leave the trampoline. You were considerate to get off when we had to go. Your friend Grace will really be excited to see you when we go to her house in a few minutes." This teaches your young child that sometimes we do things to benefit other people, reinforcing kindness and putting others first.

Now, there may be times when your child throws a barn burner of a tantrum, and no amount of pleading and cajoling is going to change things. In this case, don't threaten him or try to use reason. Stay calm. Remind yourself that at this stage, it is a preschooler's job to bump up against his boundaries, and your job to stay firm but gentle.

Don't take it personally. Keep in mind that there is no one way to deal with tantrums. It really depends on the age of the child, the mood of the tantrum (angry or frustrated versus manipulative), and any extenuating physical circumstances that may be involved, such as fatigue or illness. Be flexible and respond individually to each tantrum, carefully trying to read the situation while maintaining authority.

One day you're a superstar because you pooped in the toilet like a big boy, and the next day you're sitting in the principal's office because you said the word *poopy* in American History class (which, if you ask me, is the perfect place to say that word).

—Dav Pilkey, *Captain Underpants and the Preposterous Plight of the Purple Potty People*

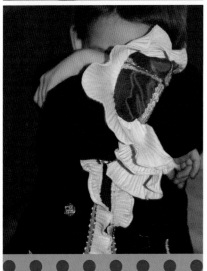

Do you know the surest way to make your child miserable? Let him have everything he wants. . .

—JEAN-JACQUES ROUSSEAU, *Emile, II*

A Note from Lesli

With our five children, how I responded
to their tantrums varied.
Our first child threw some angry 45-minute
whoppers with great regularity.
We sought the advice of a child psychologist who gave
us some effective strategies to try with her.
We learned that our daughter needed to know that we
loved her too much to let her get that out of control.

My second child was diagnosed with autism at age
two, and he found transitions to be very difficult.
His therapists helped me to redirect him with sensory
toys, such as popping balls into a hole
cut into the plastic lid of a tin. They also showed me
how to come behind him and manipulate
his arms into participating in the task that he
was rejecting, without any comment other than
congratulating him that it was done.

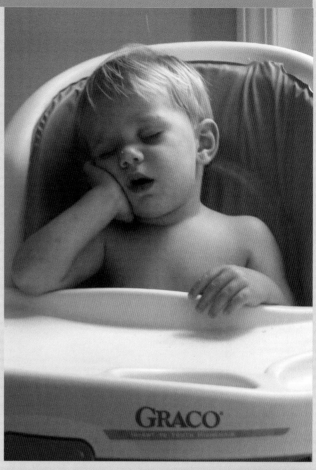

My third child never threw a tantrum until he wanted
something in a store that I wouldn't buy.
You could tell he was just trying the tantrum on for
size. I turned on my heel and made as though
I were walking out of the store. He jumped up and ran
after me. He never threw a tantrum again!

My youngest two only have a tantrum
when they are extremely tired,
and the only way to end it is to get the child to sleep.
I can usually blame those on myself!

Of course, the best way to handle a tantrum is to keep it from happening in the first place. Try to keep a sense of humor and a good attitude, making each transition to a new activity seem like a fun adventure. The car can be a spaceship, and you have to be buckled to count down to blast off! You can use old songs with new lyrics to sing your child into the next activity.

If the car seat is an issue, which is not uncommon, try building some extra time into your routine to make this a more gentle transition. Give choices such as, "What song would you like to listen to?" or "Would you like the window up or down?" Once on the road, make the ride fun by playing I-Spy or singing songs with your child.

On long errand days, consider making your preschooler a picture schedule of where you need to go. Since a young child doesn't have the same concept of time that you do (and is unable to read your day planner), she may feel a little out of control. Seeing the afternoon in picture form relieves some of this stress. Consider laminating some pictures of places you go often, such as the grocery store, the post office, the ice cream store, and so on, and then placing Velcro dots on the back of each picture. Attach Velcro to a strip of cardboard or craft foam, and place your errand pictures in order. Your child will love pulling them off as each errand is accomplished.

DIFFICULT SEASONS OF LIFE

Sometimes life is just plain hard. A tough pregnancy or illness can drain a mom, and a young child will feel that stress, too. Unemployment can cause stress and financial hardship. Caring for an elderly parent or a new baby brings new and unexpected challenges. A death can bring the world to a terrible, grieving halt.

At times like these, be flexible and set some priorities; although, sometimes you may just be in survival mode. Give yourself grace, and sincerely do the very best you can. Again, you need to look at the big picture and see that these are life lessons. Your child is watching to learn how to handle the challenges she will meet in her future.

Make a plan for the roughest days. Can a friend substitute teach for you? Can you simplify things? Just knowing that you have a pressure valve can go a long way toward keeping everything together.

Don't feel guilty about resting. There is nothing wrong with climbing into bed and inviting your preschooler to read books and color right there next to you. Because they are saved for special occasions, novelty baggies and boxes go far on days when you are not feeling up to par.

Chicken Bundles

6 cups cooked, chopped chicken

salt to taste

1 8-ounce package cream cheese

1 tablespoon chopped chives

1 bag frozen peas and carrots

2 tablespoons milk

6 8-ounce packages refrigerated crescent rolls

1 cup melted butter

2 cups crushed croutons

Mix first 6 ingredients together in a medium bowl. Preheat oven to 350 degrees. Unroll crescent rolls. Each tube will contain 4 rectangles of dough with a diagonal perforation. Press dough on each perforation so that the rectangle halves will not separate. Place about ¼ cup filling into the center of each rectangle. Fold dough over filling, and pinch edges to seal tightly. Dip each packet into melted butter and coat with crouton crumbs. Place packets on a baking sheet and bake for 20 minutes until golden brown. If you wish to freeze them, cool and wrap packets individually in plastic wrap. Place four in a gallon-size freezer bag. To serve, reheat in microwave or oven. Makes 24 packets.

Remember the basics. Stock your refrigerator with healthy snacks on a low shelf that your child can reach easily. Keep yourself and your family well hydrated and try to eat healthy. What we eat helps how we feel emotionally.

A Note from Kathy and Lesli

We make monthly trips to our local farmer's market to stock up on fresh fruit and vegetables. We divide items such as carrots, grapes, celery, and peppers and put them in snack-size baggies for quick, healthy snacks.

Visit your local farmer's market, and consider joining with other families to buy in bulk. Find out where your local restaurants are buying from, and try to get the same deal! We regularly share about 20 boxes of produce with four families to help provide organic produce for our children while keeping costs down. The children enjoy counting and sorting the fruits and vegetables for each family. Having a healthy supply on hand makes it easy to say yes when someone needs a meal or when you would like to share a bag with someone with a need. Model community spirit for your child.

Accept help. When people say, "Let me know if I can help," they usually genuinely mean it, but they may not know exactly what you need. If you are the type of person who enjoys caring for others, it can be very difficult to accept help or to verbalize exactly what you need. Consider using a friend as a go-between; friends can often see your needs before you can. A close friend can organize a care calendar to schedule meals, housework, yard work, or childcare, depending on your situation.

A Note from Kathy

When we were in the process of adopting our son from Guatemala, life became incredibly stressful. The process that was supposed to take four to six months took two-and-a-half years. The last eight months were the toughest. My husband and I took turns living in Guatemala, splitting our family completely apart. I am normally the one who enjoys helping others by watching their children and making them meals; however, I had to let go of my pride and allow others to help me and my family during this difficult season. People brought meals, watched my children for days and weeks, even cleaned my house. I don't think we would have our son today if it weren't for our friends and family who helped us along the way.

During these seasons that don't fit in the box, help your preschooler put words to his feelings. Try to create positive statements for the situation, such as, "Mommy doesn't feel well today, but maybe we can snuggle on the couch together and read a book." Try to explain things truthfully, or use books to help comfort and inform him. Sherron Killingsworth Roberts and Patricia Crawford wrote a very helpful article for *Young Children* entitled, "Real Life Calls for Real Books—Literature to Help Children Cope with Family Stressors," which offers book suggestions for almost any situation. This article may be accessed through the NAEYC website at http://www.naeyc.org/files/yc/file/200809/Crawford.pdf.

Even though things are topsy-turvy, try to maintain some mini-routines: try to make the bedtime routine the same or create some new things for the child to look forward to at certain times of the day. Compensate for the extra stressors with soothing music and relaxing stories.

I was pregnant and on bed rest with placenta previa when our son was diagnosed with autism—talk about a hard season! Between the difficult pregnancy and the burden of knowing my son would struggle with autism, I could barely function. I remember asking a friend who had experienced a difficult diagnosis for a child, "Is there ever a time that this won't be the first thing I think of when I wake up and the last thing I think of when I go to sleep?" My friend said, "No, but you will come to a kind of peace with it." She was right. It was a hard season, but only a season.

When you travel through difficult times, they can seem never-ending. Yet, eventually, the initial rush of emotion will pass, and you and your family will grow in patience and strength of character.

Chapter 9

SPECIAL
CIRCUMSTANCES

While each child is unique, there are some situations that deserve special mention. Chronic illness can lower immunity and require that a child remain isolated from other children. Therapy appointments can make it difficult for a child to attend a typical school. Homeschooling can be a good option for families who have preschoolers who are grappling with medical or developmental issues.

> You've developed the strength of a draft horse while holding onto the delicacy of a daffodil… You are the mother, advocate, and protector of a child with a disability.
>
> —LORI BORGMAN,
> "Some Mothers Get Babies with Something More"

CHILDREN WITH
SPECIAL NEEDS

Thankfully, many resources are available for home educators who wish to take the lead in helping their child reach his potential. When Lesli started homeschooling her four-year-old son who has autism, there was not much available. Now there is a wealth of information both online and through support groups. No longer do we need to haunt medical-school libraries; much research is available at our fingertips. Take advantage of the resources available to you.

My aunt Martha has Apert syndrome, which causes deformities in the face and body. As a young child I noticed the rude stares and comments from others. I asked my aunt if she was bothered, and she said, "I wish they would talk to me. I wouldn't mind if they asked me questions."

As a parent I try to use those opportunities as teachable moments. We talk openly about our differences and point out the uniqueness in us all. One day a combat veteran stood in front of us in line at the grocery store. My oldest son was interested that the man was missing his legs and began asking him what happened. The man gladly told my son about his time in the war and how he had lost both legs fighting for our country.

My very wise aunt was right. Not every person in every situation will want to tell you about her challenge or special need. However, it has been my experience that most people honor the sincere curiosity of a young child and will gladly tell their stories.

DON'T BE AFRAID OF THE LABEL

If you think your child might have an issue, don't delay getting a correct diagnosis. Early intervention is usually the key to making sure your child has the best life possible, no matter what the issue is. The idea of your child being diagnosed with any kind of disability can be disconcerting; it is easy to understand why some parents are reluctant to seek help. But, don't lose valuable time in helping your child! Particularly in the case of developmental delays and autism-spectrum disorders, the years before age five are especially critical in retraining the brain to compensate for areas that are not working as they should. Take action, see your pediatrician, and get the services your child needs.

EDUCATE YOURSELF

Once you have your pediatrician's diagnosis, try to learn as much as you can about the disorder. Call support groups and attend meetings. There is such relief in looking around a room and realizing that there are people who can understand exactly what you are dealing with. Become an expert. Do not rely on your pediatrician to tell you everything you need to know. There is no way for a typical pediatrician to keep up-to-date on the cutting-edge innovations in the treatments of every illness and disorder. Experts can be geographically or financially out of reach. Take on the role of being an expert on your child. If your child is going to speech, occupational, or physical therapy, ask the therapist if you can observe so that you can repeat the techniques at home. Ask her to help you structure a home program for your child.

CHALLENGE YOUR CHILD

Help your child learn as much as she can every day. All kids are gifted, and all kids have limitations. Be a student of your student. Continue to work on skills one at a time. Don't stress out about other people's timetables. Remind yourself of the many people who started their lives with disabilities and went on to do great things. Helen Keller was held back developmentally because she could not communicate with others. She went on to influence the world in an incredible way. Albert Einstein did not utter a word until he was four years old. Educating your child at home gives you the freedom to tailor his education. You and other members of your family are able to provide him with the one-on-one teaching that will help to compensate for the difficulties in learning. You will be able to integrate real-life situations into his education and will see which areas need enhancement to help him live his best life.

A Note from Lesli

I remember taking my son to Emory University for an evaluation when we were taking part in a genetics study. For three days he was tested and examined, while I answered thousands of questions about his life and development. At the end of those three exhausting days, I met with the director of the study to hear her advice and recommendations for Luke. I was fully prepared for her to tell me that he should be in the special-needs class at the public school. Instead, she congratulated me on a job well done and told me to keep him right where he was—at home. She said, "There are no experts on Luke [in public school]. You are the expert."

CHILDREN WITH CHRONIC ILLNESS

Homeschooling can be the ideal situation for a family grappling with medical issues. Frequent hospital stays and immunity issues make home an ideal place to learn for a child who isn't always feeling his best. For a preschooler who is facing a chronic illness, and for his caregivers, school can get pushed to the back burner, and that is okay. Much learning can take place in bed; you just need to be a little more creative. Consider the creativity of the child in Robert Louis Stevenson's poem from *A Child's Garden of Verses*:

The Land of Counterpane

When I was sick and lay a-bed,
I had two pillows at my head,
And all my toys beside me lay,
To keep me happy all the day.
And sometimes for an hour or so
I watched my leaden soldiers go,
With different uniforms and drills,
Among the bed-clothes, through
*   the hills;*

And sometimes sent my ships
*   in fleets*
All up and down among the sheets;
Or brought my trees and houses out,
And planted cities all about.
I was the giant great and still
That sits upon the pillow-hill,
And sees before him, dale and plain,
The pleasant land of counterpane.

On days when your child is well enough to play, life goes on as normal. When crisis arises, give yourself room to be flexible. Pay attention to the emotional health of your family. Chronic illness can be very isolating; use it as a chance for your family to grow closer.

On the hard days, remember your friends still care. It is a strange place to be when your life stops and everyone else's keeps moving. It can feel as though others don't care about what your family is going through. Try to remind yourself that everyone is busy; you have a new kind of unavailability due to medical appointments. Others will be conscientious in staying away if they are not feeling up to par, for fear of spreading germs. Try to use social networking sites to stay connected.

Tell people what you need. People will be ready to help if you tell them exactly what you need. Start a blog or a CaringBridge site to keep people aware of what is going on and how they can help. If you feel weird about asking, talk to a close friend, and ask her for ideas that would be helpful to your family. Your friend may suggest to others that gas cards and restaurant gift cards are a godsend for people who make frequent trips to the hospital. She may help coordinate healthy meals, trips to the grocery store, or volunteers to help with yard work.

Find a friend who will just listen. Even if a person can't directly identify with what you are going through, an open ear and open heart can be healing and encouraging. The most helpful thing anyone ever said to Lesli when she shared her son's diagnosis was, "Oh, the weight." Those little empathetic words meant more to her than anyone else's well-meaning encouragement.

Change your expectations. Every day will be different for a child struggling with health issues. Some days your child might feel too ill to accomplish much; other days he will be like a little sponge, wanting more and more. Follow your child's lead. Help him learn as much as he can every day. Preschool might be the last thing on your mind. Creative friends, especially teachers, could put some activities together for you to do when your child is up to it. If your homeschool group asks if they can help, this is a great suggestion.

This is a topic near and dear to my heart. I began to homeschool my second-grader in the waiting rooms of our local children's hospital rehabilitation center. My husband read somewhere that when you are dealing with chronic illness, you should try to make a list of "gifts the monster brought." This was one of the most helpful coping mechanisms that we had during this time.

We kept a running list on the refrigerator; we would write down names of people who wrote to us or brought us meals, or things that we were grateful for that we had taken for granted before life became so intense. I remember my husband standing in the kitchen looking over that list and saying, "This is so weird. If it weren't so awful, it would be like Christmas."

I have to say, homeschooling is one of the top gifts the "monster" of autism brought to our family. I have learned to treasure each ah-ha moment of learning, whether it is a hard-won six months spent teaching a three-year-old to place one block on top of another or a bright teenager nonchalantly bringing home a national Latin award. Victories both big and small mean so much more because of the time and effort and responsibility I have taken on.

Give your child goals to achieve. No matter how small the increments, your child can learn every day. Goal setting can take the focus off the illness and give a bit of normalcy to life. Be realistic. There are no rules for situations like this. Don't forget that time with your child is a gift. Enjoy your child. Snuggle. Read. Comfort. Now is the time to be the mama and not worry so much about being the teacher.

ADOPTING A PRESCHOOL-AGE CHILD

You might be wondering why a section on adoption is included in a book about homeschooling your preschooler. Many children adopted today are beyond the infant stage. Integrating a preschooler into an existing family comes with a unique set of challenges. Since the homeschooler sees life as school, we thought it important to include our thoughts and suggestions on this subject.

Before you adopt, begin researching the possible transition challenges of adoption. Learn about reactive attachment disorder (RAD) and the symptoms to look for. Two books we recommend are *The Connected Child* by Karen Purvis and *Building the Bonds of Attachment* by Daniel Hughes. Also, check out www.drbobmontes.com. Dr. Montes is a therapist who specializes in adoption and RAD. Many counselors specialize in RAD; find one near you. While not every adopted child needs therapy, it is good to be prepared because trials can rear their ugly heads quickly. Should you need it, there are in-house treatment facilities as well.

Take a deep breath—this might be a trying time for everyone in the family. Once you bring your adoptive preschooler home, take the time to get to know her. Spend some quality time with your new child. If this is not your only child, she will need some alone time with you. Don't be afraid to say no to outside obligations. As homeschool moms, we think we are the queens of multitasking. During this transition phase, you need to be home as much as possible. Your child needs to bond with you and your family. If too many other people are in your life on a regular basis, your child will be confused. Explain to friends that your family needs time to adjust. Have a "get to know you" celebration a few months down the road.

Establish a family routine. It is possible that your child has never experienced any type of routine. Sitting down at dinner, having a book read to her, or hearing a lullaby could all be firsts for your child. Schedule tea parties with your other children. Set up a special place in your room or other cozy area where you can connect with your children on a regular basis. Encourage your other children to share their feelings about the adoption and the transition. Journaling is a great tool for expression. Continue special routines at home that occurred before the new child arrived, and create new routines now that you

I realized at the start that whether a child is biological or adopted, one does not know all the ingredients in the package. That is what growth is all about. A child is the slowest flower in the world, opening petal by petal, revealing the developing personality within.

—ROBERT KLOSE,
professor, writer, and adoptive parent

have an additional family member. Tell lots of stories. Again, these may be firsts for your child. Tell him stories of your childhood, the adoption process, family vacations—anything that connects your child to your family.

School might look different for a season. You might feel pressure for the child to immediately catch up with his peer group. He doesn't need to! Your child needs time to adjust to this new life. Focus initially on attachment, security, social skills, and self-help skills. Your child might speak another language, and just learning to communicate and teaching him the English language will keep you busy for a while.

Build in extra time for transitions and meltdowns. Again, most adopted children have had little or no guidance. Helping your child understand boundaries and rules might add a few gray hairs to your head. Keep calm and remain steady. Consistency is a must during this phase.

Start with the basics: bathroom skills, washing hands, brushing teeth, and getting dressed. Saying *please* and *thank you,* not eating the napkin, and not shoving food in faster than the speed of light are all skills you may need to work on.

A Note from Kathy

Feed your child well. It is possible that your child has parasites, food intolerances, or food allergies. Cleaning up a child's diet can do wonders for his behavior and general health. Your child may have lived in a situation where he had no control over the food he ate or the amount he could have. Feeding your child at regular times and allowing him to have some say in his food choices will help him feel secure when it comes to food.

A Note from Lesli

One of the best things we ever did was to invite Luke's physical therapist and speech therapist into our home to give us advice on how to structure the environment to Luke's needs. It was well worth paying for an hour of their time.

I had a fantastic colorful playroom with shelves full of great developmental toys. The occupational therapist explained to me that it was wonderful but way too overstimulating for Luke's sensory issues. We changed the colorful shelves to plain white cabinets and installed a platform swing in the middle of the room. The toys were kept locked up, and we brought them out one at a time. Because he had to attempt some speech to get the toy he wanted, we challenged Luke to improve his communication skills. With only one toy to focus on, he began to play more appropriately.

Read, read, and read some more. Reading is healing to everyone. Some adopted children have never heard a nursery rhyme, "The Three Little Bears," or *Brown Bear, Brown Bear, What Do You See?*

Minimize the school work with your other children. You will probably spend so much time dealing with the transition of the new little one that you will have very little time to school your other children. If you have older children, ask them to step in and help with the younger ones. If not, maybe a homeschooling friend might be willing to send her older child over a couple of days a week for support. This season will pass and everyone will have benefitted from the more valuable thing: welcoming a child into a forever family.

ACTIVITIES

So much of what you already do at home with your preschooler encourages learning and development. We've included a wide variety of activity ideas in this section. As you nurture your child's curiosity, discover answers to questions together, and engage her in learning, you will, no doubt, come up with many more activity ideas on your own.

Children, like adults, learn best when they are interested. Our goal is to nurture children and encourage their lifelong interest in learning. These are the moments we treasure. These are the times we see glimpses of the desires and passions a child might have as an adult. We hope that the following activities will spark interest, encourage discovery, and create experiential opportunities for the preschoolers in your life.

> But knowledge which is acquired under compulsion obtains no hold on the mind . . . do not use compulsion, but let early education be rather a sort of amusement; you will then be better able to find out the natural bent [of the child].
>
> —PLATO, *The Republic*, Book VII

In your family's daily routine, you have many opportunities to develop your preschooler's skills in a number of areas:

- Self-help
- Self-confidence
- Social skills
- Health
- Nutrition
- Safety

Young children enjoy helping to clean, cook, and complete the tasks that keep the home running smoothly. Your child will develop self-confidence and a sense of belonging as he helps with the everyday tasks around your home. Invest in extra brooms, mops, dustpans, spray bottles, towels, and kitchen utensils. Include your child in chores from a young age, and he will grow up knowing that everyone works together to take care of the home.

In Chapter 5 we discussed some ways preschoolers can participate in chores and other home life activities. Here, we have included a few more ideas.

THE BATHROOM

Make brushing fun! Consider singing a silly song as your preschooler brushes her teeth, washes her face, brushes her hair, and gets dressed. You will be supporting her self-help skills and giving her a happy way to start the day. Try singing this song to the tune of "Here We Go 'Round the Mulberry Bush":

This is the way we brush our teeth,
brush our teeth, brush our teeth!
This is the way we brush our teeth,
so early in the morning!
This is the way we wash our faces,
wash our faces, wash our faces!
This is the way we wash our faces,
so early in the morning!

Continue singing, adding stanzas for each task.

Bathtime is typically playtime for most preschoolers. Young children love playing in water until they are pruny! Add to the fun with bathtub puffy paint. In a blender or food processor, place one cup of grated bar soap. Slowly add ¾ cup HOT water. Mix until it looks like thick muffin batter. Divide and add liquid water colors or food coloring. Give it to your preschooler at bathtime—you may never get her out of the tub!

Field Trip!

Use your regular visits to the dentist and pediatrician as learning opportunities. Talk with your preschooler about the people who work at those offices: nurses, receptionists, doctors, dentists, hygienists, and so on. Talk about their jobs and how they help keep us healthy. If possible and before your visit, ask your doctor or dentist to schedule an extra five minutes to explain to your child what she does in her job every day and to answer some of your child's questions.

Wash Those Germs Away

Teach your preschooler to sing "Twinkle, Twinkle, Little Star" as he washes his hands. His hands will be clean when he finishes singing the first stanza.

The Kitchen

- Set the Table: This is a preschooler favorite. Even the littlest hands can help put out napkins.
  - Create a template by tracing plates and silverware on a piece of paper to teach your child where things go on the table.
  - Store plates and silverware on a low shelf so that your child can reach them.
  - Keep colorful placemats, napkins, and napkin rings in a low drawer, and allow your child to express his creativity at the table.
- Clear the Table: For an older preschooler who can reach the counter, this is a great job. Balancing a plate with some silverware on it is actually a complex motor activity. You might want to try this with unbreakable plates at first, but it is remarkable how quickly they become confident and capable!
- Sorting: Encourage your child to sort kitchen items in any way he thinks is relevant: by color, texture, shape, size, or purpose. Ask him to tell you the characteristic he sorted by. He will be using math skills and developing his vocabulary at the same time.
- Create a family cookbook: Create a cookbook for your preschooler using a flip-style photo album. Use pictures and words to help develop those reading skills. Muffins, no-bake cookies, and trail mix are favorites among most little ones. You can even make copies of your cookbook to give as gifts.
- Learn about good hygiene practices: Wash hands before food preparation, and clean dishes in warm, soapy water.
- Let your child help you with simple food preparation. In the kitchen, you can develop her math, self-help and self-confidence, fine motor, vocabulary, and science skills:
  - measuring flour, sugar, water, or other ingredients;
  - counting ingredients or the number of people who will be eating;
  - pouring and stirring ingredients;
  - talking about the order of ingredients: "First, we put in the flour. Next, we add one egg. Then, we add another egg. How many eggs is that? One, two!"
  - talking about the states of matter: explore ice, water, and (from a safe distance) steam; notice the changes in the texture of a cake when it goes from being liquid batter to solid cake during baking, and so on.

Field Trip!

Cut out photos of the foods on your grocery list from grocery store circulars or magazines. Make a list for your preschooler by gluing those cutouts onto a piece of card stock. Your preschooler will enjoy checking off items as you shop together. Use your shopping trip as an opportunity to talk about good nutrition: "Bananas are on our list. They're really good for us because they have lots of vitamins to make us strong. Yum!"

Some grocery stores, such as Whole Foods, offer tours for homeschooled children. Check with your local grocer to find out if they are willing to offer a tour.

Vinegar Solution for Floors

Mix ½ cup distilled white vinegar with ½ gallon of water. Safe for hardwood, tile, and laminate floors.

CLEANING ACTIVITIES

Provide your child with some safe cleaning supplies and invite him to help on cleaning day! Reinforce daily upkeep by storing your child's spray bottle and some small washcloths on a low shelf. He can clean up his own messes and spills when necessary.

- **Helping Hands:** Sometimes everyone needs a little visual motivation and affirmation. Trace your child's hand on construction paper and let her cut out the shape. Each time your child helps you with a task, write it on one of the fingers. Encourage your child to fill her helping hand before the end of the day. She will proudly show it off! This also makes a great addition to the child's scrapbook or photo album.
- **Wipe It Up!** Preschoolers enjoy the job of wiping the table. Fill a dollar-store spray bottle with water and a tablespoon of white vinegar. Give your child a clean rag or paper towel to use for wiping.
- **The Clean Floor Dance Party:** This often-dreaded chore will become one of your favorites! Provide your child with a pair of white tube socks and a spray bottle of white vinegar and water. Encourage your child to squirt the hard floor with the vinegar solution. Put on your favorite dance music. Dance and skate around on that floor until it is shiny!

Helping Outside

Many jobs outdoors are a perfect fit for willing little hands. Your preschooler will be having so much fun that he won't even notice that he is learning science, math, and life skills and developing gross and fine motor skills—all at the same time!

- **Trash Collector:** Let your preschooler pretend that she is the trash collector. Let her use a wagon or a small trash bag to pick up sticks and trash in the yard.

- **Lawn Safety Patrol:** Let your preschooler help clean up the lawn to make mowing day safer. In this simple activity, he will learn in several areas: gross and fine motor skills in walking around and picking up toys and other objects, and social skills in developing a sense of responsibility for others' safety.

- **Car Wash:** This is such a fun chore on a hot day. Your child will build language skills as you identify parts and will build science knowledge by feeling the warm metal of the car and the hot pavement contrasted with the cool of the water. This often turns into What Else Can We Wash? Trikes, scooters, and lawn furniture can be cleaned as well.

Gardening

So much learning in such a simple activity! Gardening is a wonderful way to experience nature, and it provides lots of opportunities for developmental growth in preschoolers. Preschoolers' sensory systems come alive as chubby hands sift warm soil, and they develop fine motor skills by picking up tiny seeds. They learn counting as they divide the seeds into groups for planting. Their gross motor systems are challenged as they water their plants and dig. They can express creativity and use art skills making plant signs and stakes. By watering and weeding regularly, they learn routine and responsibility. They will learn plant development, an understanding of where foods come from, and will expand their palates as they try the vegetables and fruits they grow.

- **Dream Big!** One of the best parts of gardening is in the planning. Give your child a large piece of paper with outlines of your beds or planting area. Don't have room for a garden? Consider planting in large planters on a sunny patio or deck. Let your child dream about all of the flowers, vegetables, and fruits he would like to plant.

Safety First

Schedule a regular fire drill with your family. Decide on a meeting place outside, and rehearse getting there quickly and safely. For helpful tips on creating an escape plan, see http://www.firesafetycouncil.com/english/home_escape_plan.pdf.

● ● ● ● ● ● ● ● ●

Healthy Eating
Starts at Home

Plant a variety of vegetables in
your garden. Children are often
more willing to try a food that
they have grown themselves.

Colored pencils are fun for older preschoolers, because they can draw more
detail on their veggies.

- **Garden Collage:** Order seed catalogs online. Let your child cut out pictures
  and paste them onto construction-paper beds. When the time comes to
  plant, order some of the vegetable seeds your child chose.
- **Build-a-Bed:** If you are creating a planting area, let your child get those
  muscles working to help build your beds. Using child-sized tools, she can
  help by raking soil, pulling weeds, spreading topsoil, or digging holes for
  seeds.
- **Plant a Rainbow:** Read *Planting a Rainbow* by Lois Ehlert, and let your
  child plant his own rainbow garden. All you need are the seeds of plants
  that produce vegetables, flowers, leaves, or fruit in red, yellow, orange, blue,
  green, and purple—all the colors of the rainbow! If you aren't sure what will
  grow well in your area, check with your local agricultural extension service
  or visit a nursery for ideas. Here are some to start with:
  - Red or pink blooms: dianthus, pansy, begonias, petunia, verbena,
    and zinnia
  - Yellow or orange blooms: calendula, marigold, pansy, and zinnia
  - Green: green leafy plants, such as mint, basil, or margarita vine
  - Purple or blue blooms: dianthus, petunia, pansy, verbena, lavender,
    and zinnia
- **The Root of the Process:** Let your child see what happens underground.
  Fold a paper towel into quarters and dampen. Let your child place a seed
  in the center of the paper-towel square. Beans, radishes, and squash seeds
  work well for this activity. Place the paper towel into a quart-size freezer bag.
  Tape the bag to a sunny window, and wait for the seed to sprout roots. Use

different seeds and chart which ones sprout first! When the seed starts roots, you can plant it in a small container or in an egg carton until the plants are big enough to survive outside

- **Fishbowl Garden:** Place cotton in the bottom of an empty fishbowl or a large, clear glass vase. Wet the cotton with water, pouring out any extra water. Sprinkle the cotton with snap pea seeds. Cover with plastic wrap and a rubber band at the top. Place the bowl or vase near a sunny window. The seeds will sprout vines that will climb all around the bowl or vase. Add some toy jungle animals or a barrel full of monkeys, and read *The Jungle Book* by Rudyard Kipling to really spark your child's imagination!

- **Pizza Garden:** Plant onions, tomatoes, peppers, parsley, oregano, and basil in a small bed or in containers on your patio or deck. When the plants mature, use the produce to top unbaked pizza dough from your favorite market. Bake and enjoy!

- **Tea Garden:** Wouldn't it be fun to have a tea party with tea that you and your preschooler grew yourselves? You can even stitch your own tea bags out of rectangles cut from coffee filters. Delicious teas can be made from peppermint, lavender, lemon verbena, rose hips, bergamot, marjoram, chamomile, jasmine, coriander, thyme, violet, rosemary, and stevia. Check with a local garden center to learn what plants will grow well in your area.

- **Butterfly Garden:** Research which caterpillars and butterflies live in your growing region and what plants will attract them. Some common plants that butterflies love are heliotrope, Queen Anne's lace, sweet William, asters, coreopsis, coneflower, butterfly bush, nasturtium, and oregano. Plant a few in containers or in your garden, and enjoy identifying your beautiful winged visitors.

- **People-I-Love Garden:** Gardeners love to share plants! With your child, visit favorite friends, neighbors, and relatives and ask to take cuttings or plants they are willing to share. Plant these gifts in a special bed. Let your child draw pictures of the people, or laminate photos of them, to place on plant stakes. What a great place to sit and think about loved ones!

- **Sensory Garden:** This is a great idea from a book called *The Budding Gardener,* edited by Mary B. Rein. (Used with permission from Gryphon House, Inc., www.gryphonhouse.com.) In a garden plot or series of planters, grow some plants that represent the five senses:

  - **Touch:** lamb's ear (silky soft), silver sage (wooly), and teasel (spiny)
  - **Taste:** nasturtium, peas, swiss chard, mint, and other safe plants for a child to taste and explore
  - **Smell:** honeysuckle, lavender, rose, peppermint, thyme, sage, chamomile, and lemon balm
  - **Sight:** giant sunflower, poppy, zinnia, marigold, purple sage, and verbena
  - **Sound:** rattlesnake grass, bamboo, and love-in-a-mist

Encourage your child to make signs representing the five senses to mark each area. What fun for your child to take visitors on a sensory tour of your garden!

Theme Gardens

There are many wonderful books about gardening with children. We like *All New Square Foot Gardening* by Mel Bartholomew. Most libraries and bookstores have sections filled with books that offer ideas on all sorts of gardens. See what strikes your child's interest.

Is It Edible?

Teach your preschooler that he should not eat any plant or seed unless you tell him it is okay. Some plants and seeds can be toxic when ingested. If you are not sure if a plant is safe to eat, check with your agricultural extension service or pediatrician.

The scientific method involves logical steps:

- Ask a question
- Observe
- Create a hypothesis
- Test the hypothesis
- Analyze the results

Preschool-age children are natural scientists. Science exploration at the preschool level involves observation and asking lots and lots of questions about the things children see every day. Young children ask why and how questions all the time: Why does the sun come up in the morning? How do you make the color green? Why does ice melt? How does a spider spin a web? Nurture your child's natural curiosity, and encourage her to think of answers to her questions. Although her hypotheses may not be logical—or even physically possible—she will be thinking and expanding her understanding of the world. Listen to her ideas, and then find the answers with her. Ask her, "What do you think will happen if . . . ?" Read books together, explore, observe, and test your ideas. This is science!

CHEMISTRY

- **Jumping Colors!** Place about ¼ inch of whole milk in the bottom of a pie plate. Let milk settle until it is still. Place one drop each of red, yellow, blue, and green food coloring in the center. Carefully touch the food color with a cotton swab. Does anything happen? Now, place a drop of liquid dishwashing soap on the tip of the cotton swab, and try touching the color again. The colors will move wildly as the soap molecules try to join up with the fat molecules in the milk.

- **Evaporating Art:** On the driveway or sidewalk, mark off squares of pavement with wide, blue painter's tape. Encourage your children to draw masterpieces within the squares using sidewalk chalk. When they are finished, let your children spray the art with water from a spray bottle. Leave their work to dry, and come back later to see if the pictures look different. What happened to the water? Talk about evaporation and the water cycle.

- **Bubble Station:** Make bubble solution with the following ingredients.
  3 quarts water
  ⅔ cup liquid dish soap
  ⅔ cup cornstarch
  2 teaspoons baking powder
  Stir well. Tip: If you make the bubble solution in a gallon-size drink dispenser, the children can dispense their own bubbles into cups and containers. Encourage the children to try to make bubbles by creating a circle with their fingers or hands. Also, provide bubble wands or look around

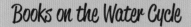

Books on the Water Cycle

Down Comes the Rain by Franklyn M. Branley
The Water Cycle by Rebecca Olien
Did a Dinosaur Drink This Water? by Robert E. Wells

your house for utensils that have circles, for example a slotted spoon or wooden spoon with a hole in the middle. We have even witnessed a child turning a piece of pine straw into a bubble wand—and it worked! The longer this solution is played with, the better the bubbles get.

- **Solid and Liquid, All in One:** One of the first scientific concepts little children explore is different forms of matter. Dump a box of cornstarch into a bucket, and mix in about a cup of water. The resulting substance is fascinating. Your child can pick it up and form a ball, then release her fist and it will run right out in a liquid mess. She can do this over and over.

- **Fizz Fun:** Baking soda and vinegar produce wonderful foaming reactions. Color little cups of vinegar with food coloring, and let your child drop in baking soda to see what happens. You can vary this activity by giving him different types of containers, pipettes, and plastic syringes.

- **What Color Is Black?** Fill small plastic cups about halfway with water. Cut a pipe cleaner in half and set aside. Using a black felt-tipped marker (not a Sharpie), make a circle of small dots in the center of a coffee filter or filter paper round purchased from a science supply store. The dot circle should be about the size of a quarter. Carefully poke the pipe cleaner through the filter in the center of the circle. Place the pipe cleaner in the water, so that it acts like a wick to pull the water up to the filter. Rest the filter flat on the top of the cup, and watch what happens. The water pulls out the colors in the black across the filter in beautiful patterns. If you experiment with pens from different manufacturers, you can see that they all have a different recipe for black!

NATURE

- **Nature Journaling:** Give your preschooler a sketch pad or notebook and pencils. Grab a blanket, maybe a snack, and head outdoors. Encourage your child to choose something to focus on and draw: a flower, a tree, a bug, or a bird. Date the journals, and your child will be creating a nature portfolio.

- **Nature Bracelet:** Taking nature walks is never the same twice. There's always something new as each season unfolds. Make a bracelet for your preschooler out of duct tape, sticky side up. Let him use the duct tape to collect small nature items as you walk: pinecones, small pebbles, flowers, and so on.

- **Nature Table:** Set up a special table or shelf in your home for displaying items your child collects, such such as pinecones, empty beehives, turtle shells, interesting rocks, and so on.

- **Nature Bottles:** Create nature bottles from items collected on your nature walks. Twigs, small pinecones, small rocks, and even dead bugs are fascinating inside a plastic bottle. Glue the top on if you have little ones who like to open and dump things.

A Note from Kathy

When we were building our home, we often took our nature journals out to our property and let the children journal the process. It wasn't long before we discovered that we had a pair of barred owls living near our new home. Below is a picture taken on the day we spotted them.

- **Name that Nature:** During your nature walk, identify the things around you. Encourage your child to notice details and ask questions. Find the answers together. Here are just a few topics to explore:
  - **Weather:** Is it rainy, sunny, warm, cold, cloudy, or windy? What causes a rainbow?
  - **Types of trees:** Try to identify the trees around you, and collect fallen leaves. Talk about how to tell how old a tree is.
  - **The landscape:** Where does that creek go? Is the land hilly or flat?
  - **Animals:** What lives in that hole in the ground or in the nest in the tree? What different insects do you see?

- **Bird Sounds:** This is a great activity for an early morning nature walk, when many birds are singing. Grab a recorder (most cell phones have one), and record the sounds you hear. When you return home, match the sound to the bird. A number of websites let you listen to birdcalls and identify the birds that make them. Just type "bird calls" into a search engine. Your children will enjoy learning about the birds in their own backyard. Beware: If you have a pet cat, be ready for it to react as you play the bird sounds!

- **Flower Power:** National Geographic's *My First Pocket Guide: Wildflowers* is a great resource for helping your little one identify flowers. After you have taken a walk to look at flowers (and maybe even pick a few), head home and let your child paint what he saw.
- **Rock Collection:** Rocks are fascinating to the young mind. Encourage your child to find unique rocks during nature walks, and help her start a collection. Display the collection on the nature table or safely stored in a special place such as a memory box (a decorated shoebox).

A Note from Lesli

My son loves collecting rocks, and he started finding heart-shaped rocks for me when he was very little. I now have a very sweet collection. We even included a few in our rock fireplace when we remodeled. He also loves to find large flat rocks and has asked me to write quotes on them. I keep these treasures on my mantle.

MAGNETS

- **Go Fishing:** This is a fun activity to do outdoors on a hot day. Fill a plastic or metal tub with water. Add nuts, bolts, paper clips, large safety pins, and magnetic letters. Make a fishing pole by tying a string to a donut-hole magnet. Let your child fish out the objects.
- **Is It Magic?** Place metal silverware, washers, giant paper clips, and so forth on top of the table. Using a large magnet, have the child move the items around from underneath the table. Kids love to surprise their friends with this activity.

WEATHER

- **Will It Blow Away?** On a windy day, collect some items from around your home, and ask your child which ones he thinks the wind will blow away. Help him make predictions and chart the outcomes on a piece of paper.
- **Weather Clothes Matching Game:** Take photos of your child wearing clothes appropriate for different types of weather, ask her to draw the pictures, or cut some out of magazines. Paste the pictures on pieces of card stock, and write different weather words on index cards (or draw symbols, such as snowflakes, water drops, a sun, and so on). Encourage your child to match the proper clothing with the weather: What do we wear in the snow? What do we wear when it is hot outside and we're going swimming?

Water Safety

Always watch your child around water. Do not leave your child unattended—even for a moment!

Making Predictions

Predicting is an important part of science. Scientists observe the subjects they study, notice the details, and then make predictions based on what they have learned through careful observation. Encourage your preschooler to make predictions: On a cloudy day, will it be cold outside? If she touches this magnet to that paper clip, will the paper clip "stick" to the magnet? What about that wooden block? Encourage her to test her predictions—she will be a scientist!

A light table is a fascinating tool for exploring science and sensory activities in new ways. While many education companies sell these light tables for hundreds of dollars, there are ways to make one cheaply at home

We have used an extra plastic bin for our sensory table and have drilled a hole in the bottom, adding a string of rope lights. We had a piece of Plexiglas cut to fit on top of the bin. Voila! Our own light table. Directions for this and for an inexpensive, portable version are in the Appendix.

- **Water Beads:** Use colored polymer water beads on your light table. Your child can explore the ways the light refracts through the different colors.
- **Cups and Colored Pieces:** Let your child stack translucent colored cups on the light table. Provide an assortment of shapes, numbers, and letters cut out of colored, translucent file folders. Cut simple shapes, such as squares, rectangles, and triangles, out of plastic file folders. Put a ¼-inch slot in each side of each shape, and your child can use the shapes to build on top of the light table. Just show her how to fit the slots together.
- **Sheer Fabrics:** Give your child a basket of tulle and other fabric scraps to layer and design with on the light table.
- **Jumping Colors:** Try the jumping colors experiment from page 116 on top of the light table. Do it in a clear plastic bin to contain any mess. The light shining through is exciting!
- **Rock and Gem Sorting:** Playing with rocks and gems on a light table makes the minerals glow and shimmer. Give your child small plastic cups and some tongs to sort the rocks with.
- **Marbles in Petri Dishes:** Encourage your child to play with centrifugal force as he moves the marbles around in the petri dishes.
- **Shaving Cream Paint:** Try painting on a light table with shaving cream, and observe how the light changes the painting!
- **Bubbles of Light:** Place bubble solution in a small cup for your child. Add food coloring, and let your child blow bubbles onto the light table. The bubbles will create beautiful patterns of color.

- **Animal Yoga:** *My First Yoga: Animal Poses* by Abbie Davies has lots of fun ideas for your child to try. Take photos of your child doing the poses, cover the photos in contact paper, and put them on a key ring. Your child can do this yoga routine every day!

- **Animal Charades:** Whenever you have to wait (at the doctor's office, for example), play Animal Charades with your preschooler. She will love seeing Mom or Dad pretending to be a tiger or a monkey!

- **Follow the Line!** Make a line of painter's tape on the floor through your house. Encourage your preschooler to follow and balance on the line. Surprise your child by making the line lead from his bedroom all the way to an outdoor picnic breakfast.

- **Freeze Tag:** This is an oldie but a goody! Your child will use her large muscle groups and learn self-control. One person is "it," the tagger. The other children run around trying to avoid being frozen (or touched) by the tagger. Once frozen, the child must stand still for 10 seconds. If your preschooler cannot count to 10 yet, you can count out loud for her until she can do it herself. Let the children take turns being it.

- **Freeze Dance:** If the weather outside is frightful, simply turn on some dance music and encourage your preschoolers to show you their best moves. Stop the music occasionally, and everyone freezes. The dancing continues when the music starts again.

- **Tap Shoes:** Tape coins at both the toe and heel portions of the bottoms of your child's shoes, and you have tap shoes! Play some lively music, and encourage your child to dance.
- **Hopscotch:** Your preschooler can play this game in so many ways, inside or outside. You can use sidewalk chalk outside or, for a permanent option on your patio or driveway, you can even paint a hopscotch caterpillar with concrete paint. Inside, you can use a permanent marker to write numbers on bubble wrap squares. Tape the squares to your floor using painter's tape. Vary the game by writing letters or shapes in the squares instead of numbers. Encourage your preschooler to call out the letter or shape before she hops.

- **Obstacle Course:** Make a picture poster of an obstacle course for your child to do. Ours went something like this:
  - Run out to the fort and go down the slide.
  - Jump on the trampoline 20 times.
  - Run all the way around the outside of the house.
  - Ride your scooter around Mom's car once.
  - Jump the hurdles (pool noodles balanced on buckets or cones).
  - Come in and have a nice snack with Mom.

- **Build a Fort:** Using pillows and blankets and furniture, make different forts. One of Lesli's fondest memories is making a fort from all the dining room chairs, couch pillows, and blankets with her cousin and then pretending it was a pirate ship.
- **Pitch a Tent:** Purchase an inexpensive pup tent, and set it up in the living room or backyard. There is a lot of movement and planning that goes into pitching a tent! Serve dinner or play a game in the tent. If you are extra adventurous, sleep in the tent with your preschooler.
- **Jump-Rope Games:** Teach your child to jump rope. Check out some books of jump rope games, such as *Anna Banana: 101 Jump-Rope Rhymes* by Joanna Cole, and ask some friends over to play!
- **Climbing Over and Under:** Help your preschooler make up an "Over, Under" climbing course using pillows, blankets, empty large appliance boxes, and anything else he can safely crawl over or under.

- **Take a Hike:** Grab your binoculars and some friends, and head for the hills. Find a trail or reasonable hill to hike. You can even put your nature journals and pencils in a backpack, and encourage your child to sketch along the way (giving Mom and Dad a chance to catch their breath).

- **Ankle Walk:** Encourage your kids to walk around the house while holding onto their ankles. This challenging activity is great for flexibility and balance.

- **Go Fly a Kite:** When you hear a windy day is on the way, grab a kite and head for an open field. You can make a simple kite with your preschooler by cutting the bottom out of a paper bag, decorating the sides, and tying string through holes punched at one open end. (For extra strength, put reinforcers around the holes.)

- **Hop, Skip, and Jump:** The next time you and your preschooler head to the mailbox or to the garden, try hopping, skipping, and jumping instead of walking.

- **Make Your Own Balance Beam:** Full instructions for this can be found in a variety of places online. If you or someone you know is handy, this is an inexpensive project that will give your preschooler hours of challenging fun.

- **Trike Path:** Using duct tape, create a trike path for your preschooler. You can make it go in circles, have arrows going in different directions, or make it go around an area in the shape of a rectangle.

- **Stump Jump:** If you have access to a fallen tree, take advantage of it by making a game for your preschooler. Have someone (or you can do it yourself) cut the tree trunk into stumps of varying sizes. Bury these stumps into the ground, making a path for your preschooler to follow by jumping from one stump to another.

- **Outdoor Bowling:** Use aluminum cans or empty plastic bottles as bowling pins and a tennis ball or golf ball for the bowling ball. Make bowling lanes with pool noodles or long pieces of wood. Encourage your preschooler to roll the ball to knock down the "pins." (Note: If your pins tend to fall over too easily, put a little play sand or water inside each one to give it a little weight.)

- **Dodge the Sprinkler:** This is a refreshing game on a hot day. Have your preschooler grab his swimsuit while you set up the sprinkler. See how long your preschooler can run back and forth dodging the sprinkler as it moves side to side. Once the game is over, your child can jump right in and enjoy the water!

- **Fat Feet for a Day:** Make fat feet by taping the lids onto two shoeboxes and cutting a slit in the top of each that is large enough for your preschooler's feet to slip through. Make a path around your house (in or out), and see how well your preschooler can maneuver her new fat feet!

- **Pop Popcorn:** Stretch out a parachute and have the children grab it firmly at the edges. Place small hollow plastic balls in the middle of the parachute, and have the children pretend to pop the popcorn by bouncing the balls around.
- **Stuffed Animals:** Invite friends over, and encourage each child to bring his favorite stuffed animal to the playdate. Place the stuffed animals in front of their owners and bounce the animals to the middle of a parachute. Just make sure each child heads home with his own stuffed animal to avoid a tearful bedtime.
- **Beach Balls:** Beach balls make a great bouncing item for parachute play. Start with one ball on the parachute, and ask the children to bounce it as hard as they can without bouncing the ball off the parachute. For more fun, place several beach balls on the parachute.
- **Waves:** Shake the parachute up and down as fast as possible to make waves.
- **Follow the Leader:** Call out different instructions, and see if the children can listen carefully and follow the directions. For example, ask everyone who is wearing red to run to the other side of the parachute. Ask everyone whose name is Henry to run to the middle of the parachute.

Parachute Play

Parachutes are fun and have wonderful play value. Bring out the parachute whenever you have friends over. You can buy a parachute online, at toy stores, or at school-supply stores.

FINE MOTOR

- **Spaghetti in the Hole:** Provide an empty, clean parmesan cheese shaker. Give your preschooler a handful of dry spaghetti noodles, and encourage her to fill the container by placing the spaghetti in the small holes of the cheese shaker. As a variation, do this activity with dry beans and a clean, empty coffee-creamer container. Of course, if your child is allergic to peanuts and other legumes, consult your pediatrician before using dry beans. When she tires of the game, have your child decorate the shaker, tape the lid shut, and turn this activity into a rain stick or maraca.

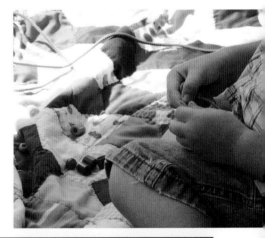

- **Drums:** Pull out the pots and pans from your kitchen for your child to use as drums, and wooden spoons for drumsticks. If just the thought of that makes you run for migraine medicine, your preschooler can make a quieter version. Provide a clean oatmeal or coffee container with lid, paint and paintbrushes, and construction paper and stickers. He can use chopsticks, unsharpened pencils, or thin wooden dowels as drumsticks. Encourage your preschooler to decorate the drum with paint, construction paper and stickers, pictures from magazines, or other art supplies.
- **Horn:** Cover the end of a paper towel roll with wax paper, and secure it with a rubber band. Punch holes in the wax paper, and your preschooler has a horn! Allow your preschooler to decorate her horn with a variety of art materials.

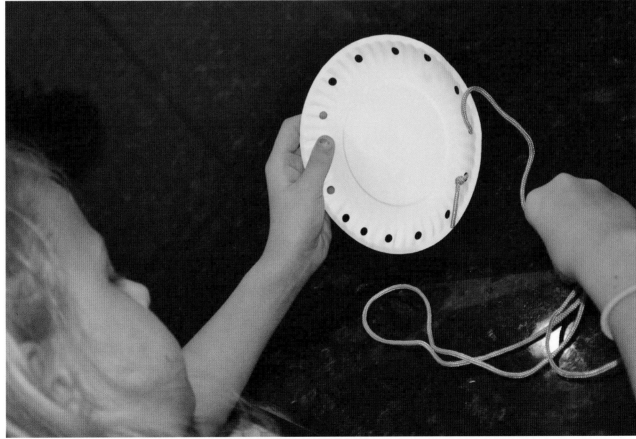

- **Toe Pick-Up:** On a large area rug, place items such as socks, pencils, plastic spoons, and paper. Have your preschooler pick up the items and place them in a container using only her toes.

- **Keys and Locks:** Provide your preschooler with a variety of keys and locks. Your child will work diligently to match the proper set. We suggest starting with a set of five locks, and once your preschooler masters those, add a few more.

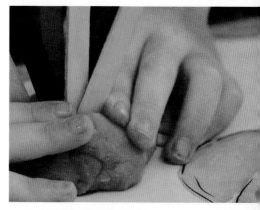

- **Wikki Stix:** These fun little wax-covered pieces of yarn have so many uses! Your preschooler can shape them, twist them, and create with them. He can make numbers, letters, and shapes with them. Available at most school supply, art supply, and toy stores, they will inspire your child.

- **Shakers:** Making maracas and shakers is easy. Fill clean, plastic soda bottles, plastic eggs, or yogurt containers with a couple of tablespoons of dry beans, rice, or unpopped popcorn. Secure the lids with adhesive or duct tape. Let your preschooler decorate the shakers with colored masking tape or duct tape, stickers, markers, and other art supplies. Play some music, and then shake 'em!

- **Clothespins and Containers:** You will need an oatmeal container or coffee can (covered with paper or otherwise decorated) and 8–10 clothespins. Your preschooler will strengthen her fine motor skills as she places the clothespins around the top of the container. Simply store the clothespins inside the container and replace the lid.

- **Kneading Dough:** Provide your preschooler with this classic sensory activity. You can give him playdough, or for a lesson in chemistry and nutrition, provide him with real bread dough.

Bread Recipe

5–6 cups of bread flour
2 cups warm water
½ cup olive oil

½ cup honey
1 teaspoon salt
3 teaspoons dry yeast

Mix warm water, oil, and honey. Add 3 cups of flour, salt, and yeast. Stir well. Add remaining flour and mix. Pour the dough onto a clean, floured surface, and let your child knead for 10 minutes, adding flour as needed. Divide dough in half, and place in two greased bread pans. Cover dough with a clean dish towel, and let rise for 20 minutes. Bake dough at 350 degrees for 20–25 minutes.

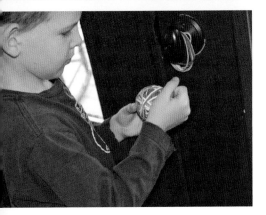

- **Transfer with Tweezers:** Give your preschooler a set of large plastic tweezers (available at school supply stores or online), a bowl of pompoms, and an empty egg carton. Encourage your child to transfer the pompoms with the tweezers into the egg carton. Develop her math skills by asking her to sort the pompoms by color or by matching the number of pompoms to a number written inside each egg-carton well.

- **Transfer with Spoons:** This is a variation on a scooping-and-pouring activity. Provide a small container full of water, dry beans, sand, or rice and an empty cup. Encourage your child to use a spoon to transfer the material from the full container to the empty one until the cup is full.

- **Nuts and Bolts:** Provide a variety of nuts and bolts in a container, and let your preschooler enjoy the work involved in matching the nut to the bolt. You probably have spare nuts and bolts in your toolbox; if not, they can be purchased inexpensively at your local hardware store.

- **Toothpick Designs:** Provide a box of toothpicks and a bag of marshmallows (grapes and pitted olives work well for older preschoolers, too) and encourage your preschooler to build and create (and make a snack). This activity also teaches math concepts of shapes, counting, and patterns.

- **Paper Clip Chain:** It doesn't get much easier than this activity. Use giant paperclips for younger kids or smaller paper clips for older kids. Encourage your child to make a chain out of the paper clips, and help her count the number of clips she uses.

- **Syringes and Basters:** Do this activity outdoors or set up a plastic tub indoors to contain the drips. Have your preschooler transfer colored water from cup to cup using plastic syringes or basters. If you provide water in two or three different colors, he can explore combining the colors to make a new color.

- **Weaving with Pipe Cleaners:** Provide your preschooler with a metal cooling rack and long pipe cleaners in a variety of colors. Encourage your child to weave the pipe cleaners in and out of the rack in any pattern he chooses. Ask him to tell you about his pattern.

Using Scissors

Learning to use scissors is a developmental skill typically gained at the preschool level. Show your preschooler how to hold the scissors properly (using left-handed scissors, if your child is left handed). If you haven't already, instruct your children that scissors are for paper only (not for hair or furniture or the baby doll's clothes).

- **Weaving with Ribbons:** Weave ribbons or pipe cleaners through plastic strawberry baskets. Encourage your child to share with others by filling the baskets with goodies and delivering them to a nursing home.
- **Sewing with Yarn:** The next time you are at the grocery store, ask someone in the meat department if you can purchase a few clean meat trays. These trays are great for sorting, painting, and sewing. Draw shapes on the trays and punch holes around the edges of the shapes. Provide your child with a large plastic needle and yarn, and let him stitch the shape. Secure the yarn on the needle so your preschooler doesn't have to worry about the yarn falling off while sewing.
- **Lacing Beads:** Lacing beads can be purchased at craft stores, school supply stores, or online. Incorporate math learning by asking your preschooler to sort the beads by color or to create a pattern with the beads.
- **Giant Noodle Lacing:** Cut two or more pool noodles into 2-inch pieces. Thread a rope through the center holes of the noodle pieces. If you cut up noodles of two or more colors, your child can make patterns out of the pieces.
- **Cutting Paper:** Let your child simply cut without having a purpose. Give your child some scrap paper, and let him practice using the scissors. If he wishes, give him some glue and additional paper, and let him create art with his paper trimmings.
- **Cutting Straight and Curved Lines:** Offer your preschooler paper with straight and curved lines drawn on with a thick marker. Encourage her to cut on the lines.
- **Cutting Shapes:** Once your preschooler has mastered cutting lines, introduce shapes traced on large paper (or printed off the computer), and allow your child to cut out the shapes. Consider providing paint or stickers and letting your child decorate the shapes.

Block Play

Block play is a classic in preschool education. Block play encourages the development of fine motor, language, cognitive, and social-emotional skills.

- **Cutting Magazines:** Provide a variety of old magazine pictures for your child to cut out. If she desires, provide some plain paper and glue, and let her make a creation or scene from the cutouts. Ask her to tell you about her picture.

- **Little People:** Children enjoy pretend play at the preschool age. Add a bucket of toy soldiers or people to your block area to extend your child's play.

- **Toy Animals:** Stretch your child's problem-solving skills by encouraging her to design spaces for her animals. Ask her to describe how the animals will get food, who their playmates will be, and where they will sleep.

- **Cars and Trucks:** We have been amazed at the roads and bridges that have been built to handle the cars and trucks in the block area. Consider offering your preschooler some duct tape or painter's tape to help him fill in areas needed as he builds.

- **Floor Puzzle:** Glue a poster to poster board using a spray adhesive (spray the adhesive outside, away from your children and pets). Take a picture of the poster for reference for your preschooler. Cut the poster board into 10 or 12 large puzzle shapes.
- **Ice-Pop Photo Puzzle:** Lay ice-pop sticks under a photo, and cut the photo into strips. Glue the photo strips onto the sticks. Provide your preschooler with a matching photo as a guide. Mix up the sticks and encourage your preschooler to arrange the puzzle to recreate the full picture.
- **Magnetic Puzzle:** Find an interesting scene or picture in a magazine, and adhere it to card stock using spray adhesive or glue. Cut the picture into puzzle pieces, and add sticker magnets to the back of the pieces. Let your child put the puzzle together on a cookie sheet or magnet board.
- **Placemat Puzzle:** Purchase inexpensive paper or foam placemats at your local dollar store. Cut the placemats into pieces and use them as puzzles for your preschooler.
- **Tangrams:** Tangrams are puzzles consisting of five triangles, a square, and a parallelogram cut from a large square. The pieces can be arranged and rearranged in countless ways. Type "printable tangram pattern" into a search engine to find a pattern. Cut the shapes out of paper or card stock, and store the pieces in a baggie. Your preschooler will love creating pictures with these shapes.

Puzzles

Puzzles are an engaging fine motor activity that also teaches math and problem-solving skills. Try making your own puzzles to add to your supply of fine motor activities. If you have two or more similar puzzles, put a different number or symbol on the back of each puzzle in case the pieces get mixed up.

- **Bean Bag Toss:** Draw numbers on pieces of card stock, and lay the cards on the floor. Encourage your child to throw the bean bags onto the numbers you call out. Older preschoolers can toss the bag onto the even numbers or the odd numbers.

- **Sorting Beach Shells:** If you take a trip to the beach, collect shells for sorting. You can have your child sort them by size, color, or shape. As your child learns to count, you can provide paper cups with numbers on them and have your child count the corresponding number of small shells into the cups.

- **Muffin Tins:** Find math counters in a variety of colors and shapes, such as animals, cars, or dinosaurs, at your local school-supply store or online. Encourage your preschooler to count with them, place the counters in patterns, or sort the counters by color or shape into muffin tins. Write numbers on small pieces of paper, and place the papers in the muffin tins. Encourage your child to place the corresponding counters in each muffin cup.

- **Roll the Dice:** Make your own big dice from wooden blocks from the craft store. Make one set with dots and one set with numbers. Younger children can count the dots or name the numbers. Then they can match the numbers. Eventually they can start counting the numbers and adding them.

- **One-to-One Correspondence with Clothespins:** Draw the numbers 1–10 on a set of small paper or plastic cups. Give your child clothespins, and ask him to pin the corresponding number of clothespins onto each of the cups.

- **Watermelon Counting:** Cut out half-circle watermelon slices from construction paper, and color large dry beans with a black permanent marker. Keep these pieces in a baggie to have as a quick on-the-go math activity. Tell your child the number of seeds to place on the watermelon slice. For a fine motor addition, have him use tweezers or tongs to take the seeds out of a cup and place them on the watermelon.

- **Small, Medium, and Large:** Give your child a nice assortment of small, medium, and large containers and matching lids. You can use little plastic juice bottles, baby food jars, spice jars, and so on. Encourage her to match the jars and tops. Talk with her as she works, using the terms *small, medium, large, smaller,* and *larger.*

- **Rhythm Sticks:** Rhythm sticks are a great tool for fine motor skills, math, and cognitive development. Buy ½-inch or thicker wooden dowels from your local hardware store. Most stores will cut the dowels for you; 8 inches in length works great. Or, consider providing your preschooler with two

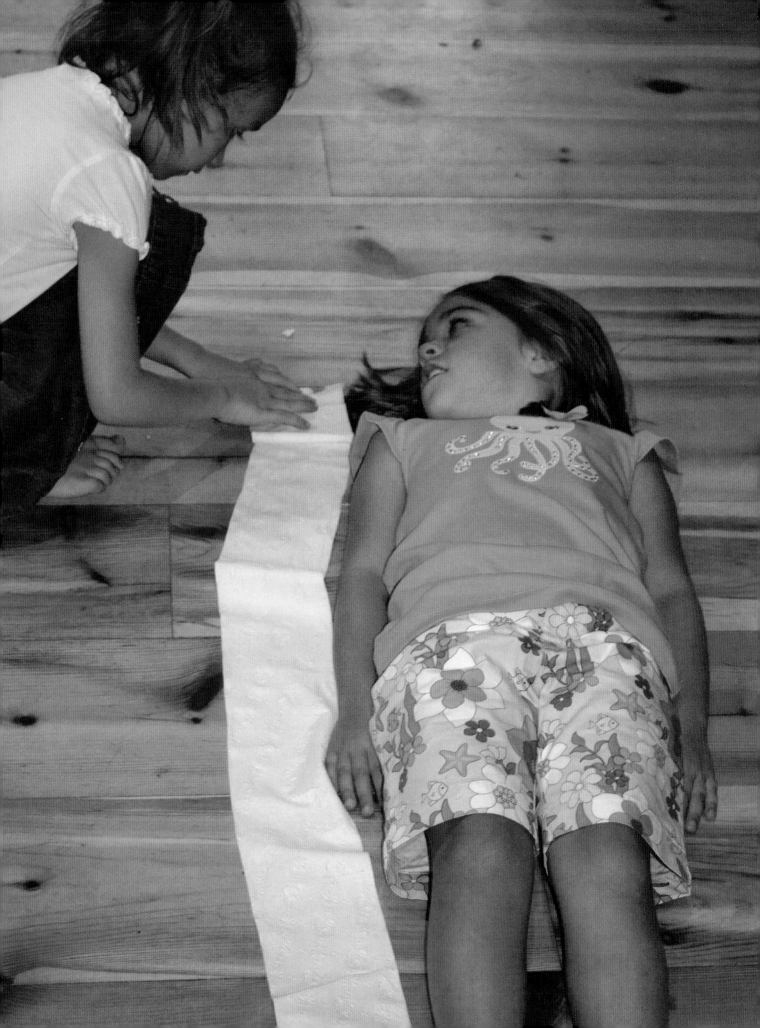

different sizes, so she can compare and contrast the noises based on the thickness.

- **File Folder Games:** These are board games that fit into manila file folders. Type "file folder games for preschoolers" in a search engine to find printable games.

- **Apple Graphing:** Buy several varieties of apples, and then cut them into pieces. Make a simple graph, listing the names of your family members down the left-hand side and the types of apples you are testing across the bottom. Let each family member try the apples and tell you which one he or she prefers. Ask your preschooler to color in the favorite choice of each person. This is a tasty way for your preschooler to learn that apples come in many shapes, sizes, and flavors.

- **Count Your Own Snack:** Make five tented cards out of construction paper (fold the cards in half to make little tents). Number the cards by fives: 5, 10, 15, 20, 25, and stand them in a row. In front of the cards, place baggies or cups of trail-mix makings: candy-coated chocolate (5), mini marshmallows (10), whole-grain cereal (15), oat cereal (20), and raisins (25). (Use the trail-mix ingredients that your family prefers.) Give your preschooler an empty bowl, and allow her to count out her own snack.

- **TP Measuring:** Teach estimating and measuring with nonstandard units. Let your child guess how many toilet-paper squares it will take to equal his height. Then, ask him to lie down on the floor, and measure him. Tear off the right number of squares. Next, lie down and let him measure you. Let him measure Dad, the dog, the cat, the table, and so on. Compare the different measurements, and talk with your child about who is tallest and shortest. Let him place the toilet paper lengths in order from tallest to shortest.

- **Shoe Measuring:** Measure how many steps it is between two points, using kid shoes and adult shoes. Measure how many steps to the sidewalk, how many steps from the bed to the breakfast table, and so on. Use the measurements to help your child make a map.

- **Make Your Own Pattern Strips:** Cut different colors of construction paper into 2-inch strips. Create patterns for your child to copy, and then have her make a pattern for you to copy.

- **Dot Marker Numbers:** Washable dot or bingo markers are great for math, art, and fine motor, and you can use them all kinds of ways. Write numbers on paper and have your preschooler make the corresponding number of dots. If your child is just learning numbers, make the correct number of circles with a pen and have her place a dot in each circle. Then, count the number of dots with her.

- **Shape Treasure Hunt:** Go on a hunt in your house for circles. Take photos of the items you find and make a circle book for your child. Another time, go on a square hunt or a hunt for rectangles. Make books of photos of each shape.

- **Make a Counting Book:** Take a photo of your child holding one stuffed animal, then two flowers, three toy cars, and so on. Glue the photos onto

Recognizing Patterns

Recognizing simple patterns is an important math skill. Provide a variety of patterns for your child: AB-AB, ABBA-ABBA, ABA-ABA, AAB-AAB, and so on. Encourage your child to copy your patterns and then to create patterns for you to copy. For example, you might make a red-blue-blue (ABB) pattern with blocks; or you could make a dog-cat-dog (ABA) pattern from your child's toy animals.

card stock, and slip each card into a sandwich-size baggie. Seal the bags, punch holes in one side, and tie the pages together with yarn. Cozy up with your preschooler and "read" the book together.

- **Adding It Up:** Purchase two-color counters online or at a school-supply store. Toss five of them onto a table. Some will come up one color, and some will come up another color. Count the number of each color with your child; for example, three yellow ones and two red ones. This activity will help your child to see that 3 + 2 = 5 and 2 + 3 = 5. Toss the same five counters again, and recount.
- **Paper Chain Countdown:** Make a colorful paper chain out of strips of construction paper. Write a number on each link, beginning with the number one. Use the chain to count down to an upcoming event, such as a family vacation or a visit from Grandma.

- **Opposites Hunt:** As you go through the day, make an effort to point out concepts that are opposites, such as big and little, open and closed, many and few, far and near, first and last, inside and outside, and narrow and wide. Pretty soon, your child will be pointing them out to you!
- **Color in the Bag:** Purchase colored paper gift bags, and choose one color for your preschooler to use. Let your child hunt for items around your house that are the same color as the bag, and encourage her to place the items in the bag. Expand the activity by giving her two colors to hunt for, and then three.
- **Estimation Jar:** This activity can be done over and over in a variety of ways. Put any type of item you can think of (paper clips, candy, buttons, corks, doorknobs, cut straws, and so on) in any type of clear container you have

on hand. Small mason jars and baby food jars work well. Encourage your preschooler to guess how much is in the jar, and then count out the contents together. Expand this activity by comparing two jars of equal size that contain two different types of items. Graph the contents of each jar. For example, a mason jar may fit 35 dry beans but the same size jar may fit only three blocks.

- **Pattern Blocks:** Pattern blocks offer so many ways for your preschooler to explore creating with shapes. As she works, talk with her about the shapes she is using. Purchase pattern blocks online or at school-supply stores, or type "pattern blocks template" into a search engine to find printable patterns online. Just cut the shapes out of sturdy paper.
- **Memory Games:** Color index cards in a variety of colors, and cut the cards in half. Mix the cards up, and place them facedown on a table. Take turns with your preschooler, flipping two cards over until you make a match. Play

until all the matches have been made. Vary the game by matching shapes or matching numbers and dots.
- **Shape Collage:** Cut large shapes out of construction paper, and give them to your preschooler along with some glue and a large piece of plain paper. Encourage him to make shape-collage art.
- **Ice-Pop Stick Shapes:** Give your preschooler colored ice-pop sticks and have her create shapes. She can glue the sticks together if she wishes.

Little Entrepreneurs

Preschoolers are developmentally ready to recognize and distinguish different coins and to understand how much the coins are worth. Teach children how to responsibly handle money, and let them help you when you pay for items at the grocery store.

- **Object Match:** Collect items from around the house, and trace them on a large piece of paper. Give your preschooler the items, and ask him to match them to the outlines. Here are few items that are fun to trace: a deck of cards, a plate, a coin, scissors, a pencil, and a tube of toothpaste.

- **Save, Spend, Share:** Cover three tall potato-chip cans with scrapbook paper or plain paper that your child can decorate. Label them *save, spend,* and *share.* When your child receives money for a birthday or earns money for special chores, have her divide the money among the three jars. Encourage her to use her own money to purchase small items or to donate to a cause she would like to support. This will develop lifelong habits in stewardship and generosity.

- **Mom's Store:** Consider making your own store in a closet or cupboard in your house, with little items for your preschooler to purchase. Let your child earn Mom Money (construction paper scrip) to purchase small toys and games, books, or other leisure-time items. Clearly label the items with how much they cost. This will help your child to see the relationship between how much items cost and how hard someone has to work to afford them.

- **Lemonade Stand:** This childhood rite of passage is a terrific eye-opening lesson in running a business! Crafting the stand itself, making invitations for neighbors and friends, figuring out the amount of needed supplies, salesmanship—this time-tested activity is loaded with fine motor, language, math, and social-emotional skill-building opportunities.

- **Bake Sale:** Make cookies, brownies, or muffins with your child, and have a bake sale! Consider donating your proceeds to a worthy cause.

- **Stationery Sale:** Place a dollop of shaving cream in a tray or rimmed cookie sheet. Add drops of food coloring or tempera paint, and give your preschooler some fun utensils to use to make patterns: plastic fork, marbles, and so on. Let your child place a clean piece of card stock over the shaving cream color, making a print. Squeegee off the extra, and let the paper dry. Mom or Dad can iron the paper if it starts to curl. Cut the paper into rectangles, and attach them to notecards. Tie a set with ribbon, and your child can sell them or give them as gifts. They even smell nice, if you use scented shaving cream!

- **Vegetable Stand:** If you have the space, plant a vegetable garden and let your child grow some veggies to sell. Most people are thrilled with the idea of purchasing fresh produce from someone they know and are even more thrilled to know that a little one is getting some business experience as well.

- **Garage Sale:** If the toy clutter is building up on you, ask your children if they would like to have a garage or yard sale. Let your child decide what he will sell; do not force him to sell something that he wants to keep. Let your preschooler help you make signs, organize the items, and set up the tables on sale day. Your child will learn about bargaining and negotiating and will be happy to have a little money in return for toys he no longer uses.

- **Trading Party:** Let your child help you organize a trading party with other families. She can help make invitations, and you can talk together about what the rules should be and how the party should be organized. This can be done on a small or large scale and is a great way to show your child that trading and bartering are a vibrant part of the economy. A trading party can work well with toys, dress-up costumes, books, or clothes.

Field Trip!

Call your local bank manager, and ask if the branch will host a field trip for homeschoolers. Most are willing to educate children about how a bank operates. Children can talk to a teller, see where the money is kept, and look at an ATM up close. See what numbers on the ATM your child recognizes. Let the children examine the envelopes, deposit slips, pens, and information brochures they find in the bank. The manager may even give them a few blank forms so they can play Bank at home. Follow up the visit with a thank-you note, and try setting up some banking supplies in your dramatic play area.

- **Reading Spot:** Make an inviting place to read. Buy a plastic wading pool, and fill it with comfy pillows, blankets, and stuffed animals. Keep a basket of books nearby, and you have a great reading spot for your preschooler. We have listed ideas using some of our favorite children's books.
- *Big Red Barn* **by Margaret Wise Brown:** Help your preschooler learn about life on a farm. Encourage her to build a little farm using blocks or building toys, hay or straw, toy farm animals, toy trucks and tractors, and little toy people to work on the farm.
- *An Island Grows* **by Lola Schaefer:** This beautiful book takes the children on a journey as an undersea volcano becomes a beautiful, lush island. Expand the learning by creating a volcano with your child. Cover a plastic two-liter bottle with salt dough. Shape the dough around the soda bottle, and let the dough harden overnight.

When you are ready to watch your volcano erupt, set the bottle on a large cookie sheet or in a plastic tub. Funnel ⅓ cup baking soda into your bottle. Mix a few drops of red food coloring with 1 cup of vinegar, and slowly pour the colored vinegar into the bottle. Stand back and prepare to be the coolest mom in town.

Salt Dough

1 cup salt
1¼ cup water
3 cups flour
Add salt to water, stirring until dissolved. Add flour, 1 cup at a time until dough is pliable and smooth.

Open Up New Worlds

Almost any children's book offers ways to extend the learning. Here, we offer ideas to get you started. As you and your preschooler explore books together, you will think of many more.

- *Make Way for Ducklings* by Robert McCloskey: Create a large nest with blankets, and snuggle in tight as you read this book to your preschooler. For more fun, provide your child with a variety of materials, such as yarn, pine straw, string, ribbon, or shredded paper to use to build his own nest.
- *Diary of a Worm* by Doreen Cronin: This lively book walks a child through the life of a worm. Create a worm habitat with your child. Gather the following items:

2-liter, clean plastic bottle	Dark construction paper
16- or 20-ounce plastic water bottle	Soil
Water	Sand
Scissors	Oatmeal
Tape	Worms

Adult only: Cut the top off the 2-liter bottle. Tape the edges of the bottle to keep everyone safe.

Fill the smaller bottle with water, and place it in the middle of the two-liter bottle to keep the worms on the outside of the container, for better viewing. Layer the larger container with soil, sand, construction paper, and oatmeal until about three-quarters full. Go on a worm search in your yard, or (if you live in an area where earthworms are scarce) purchase some earthworms from a bait shop. Add several worms into your habitat and watch what happens.

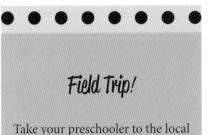

Field Trip!

Take your preschooler to the local public library. Let her meet the librarians, and walk around with her to show how the books are organized. Let her get her very own library card, and help her check out books to take home and read with you. Then, use your library cards often!

- *Chicka Chicka Boom Boom* by Bill Martin, Jr. and John Archambault: Make a *Chicka Chicka Boom Boom* tree. Cover a Styrofoam cone with brown construction paper. Stick leaves (either real or artificial) into the foam trunk. Add foam letter stickers to the trunk of the tree. Foam letter stickers are available online or at school-supply stores.

- *Goodnight Moon* by Margaret Wise Brown: Use this book to start a bedtime routine, or add it to your existing routine. For fun, add *Good Night, Gorilla* by Peggy Rathmann, too. Expand the learning by reading about real gorillas. Seymour Simon's *Gorillas i*s an informative book for children.

- *The Very Hungry Caterpillar* by Eric Carle: This book reinforces counting skills and has terrific art that inspires children. Expand the learning by making a chalk caterpillar hopscotch on your driveway or patio. Consider getting some real caterpillars to watch as they create chrysalises and hatch into butterflies. Butterfly garden sets are available online or at school-supply stores.

- *Wilfrid Gordon McDonald Partridge* by Mem Fox: This book is all about memories. Create a memory box with your child. Cover a shoe box with contact paper or construction paper and stickers. Use the memory box as a special place for your child to store treasures, such as rocks, shells, pictures, leaves, and so on.

• • • • • • • • • •

A Note from Kathy

Before my Aunt Nell died, I asked her to write down some stories from her childhood. I wanted to hear how life was for her and her 10 siblings (including my father). One of my favorite stories is about books. She writes, "When I was young we didn't have much money so I would take my book, usually my geography book, and I would go outside and climb a tree. I would read my book and imagine I was going to all of the places I read about." Books really are windows into the world.

● *Our Granny* **by Margaret Wild:** The creative text and imaginative illustrations will make this book a family favorite. Provide your preschooler with art materials and encourage him to paint a picture for a grandparent or another special person. Ask your preschooler to tell you the things that make this person special, and write down what he shares. Put the art and the special list in an envelope, and mail it to your preschooler's special person.

- *Green Eggs and Ham* by Dr. Seuss: The natural activity to do with your preschooler is to cook eggs tinged green with a little food coloring and to serve them up with a big slice of ham.
- *My Many Colored Days* by Dr. Seuss: This book helps a child identify her feelings by associating moods with colors. Let your preschooler create her own mood book, choosing a name and all. You can take photographs of her displaying her many moods or let her illustrate the book. She can tell you the words to write.
- *Brown Bear, Brown Bear, What Do You See?* by Eric Carle: The predictable text helps a child feel confident as he "reads" the book along with you. The art in this book is made of beautiful tissue-paper collages. Provide your preschooler with different colors of scrap tissue paper, construction paper, and glue, and let him explore creating a collage in any way he likes.

- *If You Give a Pig a Pancake* by Laura Numeroff: Plan to read this delightful book under or on a parachute while your child enjoys pancakes, complete with maple syrup (in her pajamas, of course!).
- *Cloudy with a Chance of Meatballs* by Judi Barrett: This silly, silly book is fun to act out. Give your child a handheld strainer or sand bucket, and let the food rain down. You can toss berries, marshmallows, popcorn, raisins, pretzels, and so on.
- *Animals in Winter* by Henrietta Bancroft: This is a lovely nonfiction book written specifically for preschoolers. Help your preschooler build a cave out of blankets, pillows, and a chair or two. Then let her pretend to hibernate as you read together.

- *Little Cloud* by Eric Carle: This is a great book about finding shapes in clouds. Make up a batch of cloud dough (see page173) and form your own. Help your preschooler take photos of different kinds of clouds, and make a book that identifies each type.

- *What Moms Do Best/What Dads Do Best* by Laura Numeroff: Half of this book is about moms, and the other half is about dads. Have your child journal or draw pictures about his parents and what he thinks they do best.

- *Caps for Sale: A Tale of a Peddler, Some Monkeys, and Their Monkey Business* by Esphyr Slobodkina: A hilarious story of a peddler who tries to outwit a band of monkeys. Your preschooler will love the silly story and the language repetition. Play a game of hat hide-and-seek: Hide hats around your house, and let your preschooler find them. Then, let her hide the hats, and you seek them.

- *Guess How Much I Love You* by Sam McBratney: You might need to grab some tissues before reading this one to your child. As moms we know that it is impossible for our children to understand just how much we love them. Make love notes to family members, telling them how much they are loved. Your preschooler can decorate these notes with heart stickers and stamps

Record Your Favorite Books

Record yourself reading your preschooler's favorite books. There are lots of free voice-recorder apps available. If you burn a CD or use your MP3 player, your preschooler will be able to listen to his favorite books anytime.

Building Communication and Emergent Literacy Skills

Reading with your preschooler is an important way to build his vocabulary and emergent literacy skills. But, you can do even more! We've included lots of simple activities that will help you develop your preschooler's alphabet knowledge, phonological awareness, and comprehension.

● *Bread and Jam for Frances* by Russell Hoban: Frances is a very picky eater. Your preschooler will love reading about how she finally discovers that eating a variety of foods is a good thing! Consider making some fresh bread with your preschooler (we've included a recipe in this book on page 135). Enjoy your bread with jam as a yummy snack.

- **Alphabet Picture Book:** Let your preschooler take pictures of things around your home that start with each letter of the alphabet. Help her use those photos to create her own alphabet book. Encourage her to write each letter all by herself.

- **My Favorites Book:** Take pictures of your child wearing his favorite outfit, eating his favorite food, reading his favorite book, playing with his favorite toy, watching his favorite movie, hanging out with his favorite friend. Let him tell you about each photo, and write what he says as you use the pictures to create a book. This is a fun one to do each year!

- **When I Grow Up:** Ask your child all kinds of questions about what she thinks life will be like when she grows up. What will she do? Where will she live? What will she eat? How late will she stay up? What kind of pet will she have? Will she drive a car? What kind? Encourage her to draw or cut out pictures to create a book showing her predictions. Write her predictions on each page.

- **What Would Happen If?** Play this imaginative game anywhere. Ask your preschooler questions such as, "What would happen if we could fly?" "What would happen if we had gills like fish?" "What if all the monkeys in *Caps for Sale* came to live at our house?" Let your preschooler make up "what if" questions, and have fun imagining the possibilities.

- **Name Recognition Game:** Write family members' first names on card stock. In a sensory bin filled with sand or dry beans or rice, hide the names and the corresponding magnetic or foam letters to spell them. Encourage your preschooler to find the letters to spell the names. You can even add pictures of your family members for him to match with the names. Expand this for older preschoolers by matching names of animals with the corresponding letters and small plastic animals.

- **Sensory Writing:** Any time you can put a sensory experience into a language arts activity you get a double bang for your buck! Let your child write letters with her finger in shaving cream or fingerpaint. Let her write with dry-erase markers on a mirror.

- **Sandy Alphabet:** Cut out 5-inch-high letters of the alphabet from card stock or cardboard. Spread glue on the letters and sprinkle them with play sand. When they dry, you will have a tactile alphabet for your preschooler to explore. Encourage him to trace the letters with a finger, feeling the sandy sensation.

- **Letter of the Day:** Choose a letter of the day, and look for objects with your preschooler that start with that letter. For example, if you focus on the letter B, you could point out /b/ /b/ bananas at the grocery store, /b/ /b/ Bobby who lives down the street, and /b/ /b/ bathtime. Make sure you read /b/ /b/ books!

- **Playdough Letters:** Roll playdough into long snakes and form them into letters. Seeing the letters in 3-D is especially beneficial to a young child.

Homemade Playdough

1 cup water
1 tablespoon vegetable oil
½ cup salt
1 tablespoon cream of tartar
food coloring (optional)
1 cup all-purpose flour

Combine the first four ingredients, and add a few drops of food coloring if desired. Heat in a saucepan over medium-low heat until the mixture is warm. Remove from heat and add flour. Stir until combined. Turn out on wax paper and knead until smooth. Store in an airtight container.

SONGS, RHYMES, CHANTS, AND FINGERPLAYS

Song lyrics are poetry. Use music, poems, chants, and rhymes to teach your preschooler about rhythm, syllables, and letter sounds. There are so many resources for children's songs, rhymes, chants, and fingerplays. We've included a few of our favorites here. We've also listed several books and websites in the Appendix.

- **"Twinkle, Twinkle, Little Star":**

  Twinkle, twinkle, little star,
  How I wonder what you are.
  Up above the world so high,
  Like a diamond in the sky.
  Twinkle, twinkle, little star.
  How I wonder what you are.

- **"Five Little Hot Dogs":** This is fun to do with a play skillet and plastic hot dogs. Emphasize the rhythm by clapping or tapping your knee.

  Five little hot dogs frying in the pan.
  The grease got hot, and one went BAM! (yell, "Bam!" and clap hands)
  Four little hot dogs frying in the pan. (take out one hot dog)
  The grease got hot and one went BAM! (yell "Bam!" and clap hands)
  Continue with three, two, and one.
  No little hot dogs frying in the pan.
  The grease got hot, and the pan went BAM! (yell "Bam!" and clap hands)

A Note from Kathy

Our oldest son wanted "Twinkle, Twinkle, Little Star" sung to him every night for the first few years of his life. Before his verbal skills were developed he would just cry, "Upa, upa!" at bedtime. At times, my husband got so tired of singing this song, he just would make up his own lyrics.

Music Book

Cut and paste the words to a variety of songs, nursery rhymes, and fingerplays on note cards. Punch holes in the note cards and fasten them together on a key ring. Keep your music book handy.

● **"Herman the Worm":** Children become positively giddy as they anticipate this fingerplay's ending.

Sitting on the fencepost,
Chewing my bubble gum, (make smacking sound with lips)
Playing with my yo-yo, (pretend to use yo-yo)
And along came Herman the Worm.
And he was this big. (hold hands close together)
I said, "Herman, what happened?"
He said, "Uh, I ate a mouse."
Sitting on the fencepost,
Chewing my bubble gum, (make smacking sound with lips)
Playing with my yo-yo, (pretend to use yo-yo)
And along came Herman the Worm.
And he was this big. (hold hands farther apart)
I said, "Herman, what happened?"
He said, "Uh, I ate a cat."

Continue in this manner, each time naming a larger animal that Herman ate and holding your hands farther apart.

Sitting on the fencepost,
Chewing my bubble gum, (make smacking sound with lips)
Playing with my yo-yo, (pretend to use yo-yo)
And along came Herman the Worm.
And he was this big. (hold hands very close together)
I said, "Herman, what happened?"
He said, "Uh, I burped!"

● **"Itsy Bitsy Spider":** Emphasize the rhyming words in this classic fingerplay. Not sure of the hand motions? Just type "Itsy Bitsy Spider hand movements" into a search engine to find photos and videos to show you how, or make up your own!

The itsy bitsy spider went up the waterspout.
Down came the rain and washed the spider out.
Out came the sun and dried up all the rain.
And the itsy bitsy spider went up the spout again.

For more fun, sing in a slow, deep voice: "The big, enormous spider . . ."

● **The Alphabet Song":**
(Sung to the tune of "Twinkle, Twinkle, Little Star.")

A B C D E F G
H I J K L-M-N-O-P
Q R S
T U V

W X Y and Z
Now I know my ABCs.
Next time, won't you sing with me?

- "Head, Shoulders, Knees, and Toes": Touch each body part as you sing.

  Head, shoulders, knees, and toes
  Knees and toes.
  Head, shoulders, knees, and toes
  Knees and toes.
  And eyes and ears and mouth and nose.
  Head, shoulders, knees, and toes
  Knees and toes.

- "Bingo": Reinforce listening skills and rhythm, and sing it loud!

  There was a farmer who had a dog,   *There was a farmer who had a dog,*
  and Bingo was his name-o.   *and Bingo was his name-o.*
  B-I-N-G-O   *(clap)-I-N-G-O*
  B-I-N-G-O   *(clap)-I-N-G-O*
  B-I-N-G-O   *(clap)-I-N-G-O*
  and Bingo was his name-o.   *and Bingo was his name-o.*

  Continue in this manner, replacing one more letter in *Bingo* with a clap each time, until you clap five times instead of spelling the dog's name.

- "Old MacDonald": Be prepared to name every animal you've ever heard of as you enjoy singing this song with your child.

  Old MacDonald had a farm,   *Here a quack!*
  E-I-E-I-O!   *There a quack!*
  And on his farm he had a duck,   *Everywhere a quack, quack!*
  E-I-E-I-O!   *Old MacDonald had a farm,*
  With a quack, quack here, and   *E-I-E-I-O!*
      a quack, quack there!

  Continue singing, changing the animal and animal sound each time: cow, horse, chicken, moose, elephant. (Old MacDonald has a really interesting farm!)

- "Five Little Monkeys": support counting backward and number sense with this silly song.

  Five little monkeys sittin' in a tree,   *One little monkey sittin' in a tree,*
  Teasing Mr. Alligator, saying,   *Teasing Mr. Alligator, saying,*
  "You can't catch me!"   *"You can't catch me!"*
  Along came Mr. Alligator, quiet as   *Along came Mr. Alligator, quiet*
      can be,   *as can be,*
  and CHOMP!   *and CHOMP!*
                                          No little monkeys sittin' in a tree!

  Continue singing with four, three,
      and two.

ART AND SENSORY

Art at the preschool age is about the process instead of the product. Give your preschooler all sorts of materials to explore, and stand back! Young children can lose themselves in the sensation of swirling fingerpaint around, molding clay, or gluing small items on paper. Your preschooler will love creating scribbles and marks with crayons or markers or colored pencils. Let your preschooler have lots of time to explore without a specific product in mind.

Designate places in your home to display your preschooler's art. Low shelves, frames, and creative hanging stations will add beauty to your home and show your preschooler that you value her work.

Sidewalk Chalk and Paint

Sidewalk chalk is readily available, but if you're feeling creative, you can make your own chalk and sidewalk chalk paint. For the chalk, mix 1 cup water and 1 cup plaster of Paris with 2 or 3 tablespoons of powdered tempera. Pour the mixture into muffin tins, silicone molds, ice cube trays, or toilet paper tubes lined with waxed paper, and let it dry.
For sidewalk chalk paint, mix ½ cup water and ½ cup cornstarch. Add food coloring until you get the color you desire.

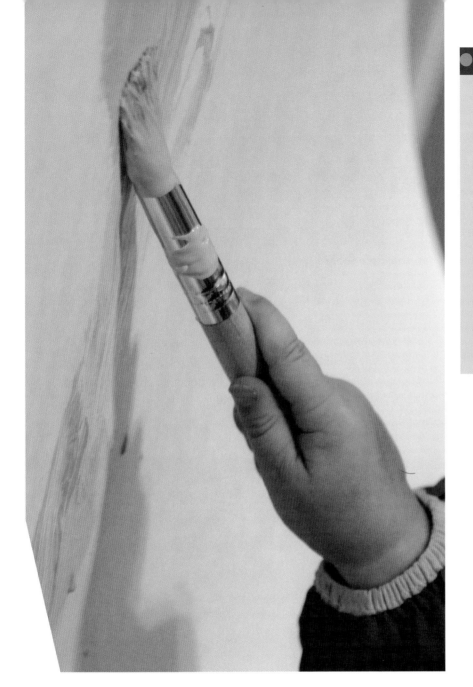

Take It Outside!

Art explorations can be messy! Whenever possible, set up art materials for your preschooler outside. Fresh air is good for you and your child, and natural light is wonderful. When she is finished creating, hose down the art area—and your child, if necessary!

PAINTING

- **Make a Scene:** Help your child draw a scene he can lie down in. Take a photograph, and consider making cards out of the photos for grandparents
- **Draw Your Shadow:** In the morning, trace the outline of your preschooler's shadow, and let her trace yours. Come back at various times during the day and stand in the same spot. Trace your shadows and notice how the shadows change as Earth moves around the sun.
- **Fizzy Paint:** Add a box of baking soda to your sidewalk chalk paint. After your child is done painting, give him a spray bottle of vinegar. His creations will fizz and bubble when he sprays them with the vinegar!

Favorite Puffy Paint

1 cup salt

1 cup flour

1 cup water

food coloring or powdered tempera

Stir first three ingredients together, and divide among cups. Add food coloring or powdered tempera.

Fingerpaint

Fingerpaint gives preschoolers opportunities to explore color, shape, and texture. Your child will develop her social and language skills as you talk with her about her creations and impressions. Fingerpainting is wonderful for developing fine motor skills and eye-hand coordination. Let your preschooler fingerpaint in a variety of places: on paper, windows, cookie sheets, bathtubs, and easels.

- **Puffy Paint:** Let your preschooler use squirt bottles or cake-decorating tubes and tips to make all kinds of creations.

- **Make Me, Bake Me Puffy Paint:** Mix 1 cup flour, 3 teaspoons baking powder, and 1 teaspoon salt. Add water until the mixture has a thick pouring consistency. Let your preschooler paint with the mixture. When the art is made, put it in the microwave for 30 seconds, watching it carefully! The paint will puff as the baking powder activates.

- **Homemade Fingerpaint:** Mix ½ cup cornstarch, ½ teaspoon salt, 3 tablespoons sugar, and 2 cups cold water with a whisk in a saucepan. Stir constantly over medium-low heat for 15–20 minutes until thick. Remove the mixture from the heat, and divide it among muffin tins or dishes. Add food coloring to make the desired colors.

- **Bathtub Fingerpaint:** Mix 1 cup baby wash with 1 tablespoon of cornstarch. Divide among muffin-tin cups, and color with food coloring or liquid water colors. Your preschooler will love exploring the soapy colors!

- **Homemade Liquid Watercolors:** Mix together 4 tablespoons of baking soda, 2 tablespoons of white vinegar, 1 teaspoon of light corn syrup, and 4 tablespoons of cornstarch. Divide the mixture into small paint jars (sold at craft stores), and stir in paste food coloring.

- **Homemade Solid Watercolors:** Mix 3 tablespoons each of baking soda, cornstarch, and white vinegar. Wait for the fizzing to stop, and add 1½ teaspoon of corn syrup. Pour into a clean, empty egg carton or paint wells, and mix in food coloring. Let the paint dry for three hours, and pour off any excess liquid.

- **Watercolor Butterflies:** Encourage your child to drop liquid watercolors onto coffee filters to make beautiful designs. Gather the coffee filter in the center and pinch inside a clothespin to make a lovely butterfly.

- **Paint to Music:** Play a variety of music for your child, and ask him to paint with colors and shapes that "look like the music sounds." When he is finished, ask him to tell you about his creation.

- **Crayon Resist:** Encourage your preschooler to draw a secret message or picture with a white crayon on white paper. When she paints over the crayon with liquid watercolor, the secret picture will appear.

- **Cornstarch Fadeaway:** Fill a large tray with two boxes of white cornstarch. Smooth it over with a large hair pick or pasta rake. Give your preschooler spray bottles filled with liquid watercolor, and let him create pictures or use stencils to make designs. Then, let him rake his design and watch it disappear. He can do this over and over again.

- **Tongue Painting:** This is a favorite activity from *101 Easy, Wacky, Crazy Activities for Young Children* by Carole Dibble and Kathy H. Lee. Place a tablespoon of corn syrup or agave nectar on a small paper plate, add food coloring or berry juice, and let your child paint using her tongue! Your preschooler will ask to do this activity over and over again. (Used with permission from Gryphon House, Inc., http://www.gryphonhouse.com.)
- **Easel Art:** Give your child big paper on an easel, along with some tempera paint and brushes. There is something about painting on an easel that makes one feel like a real artist.
- **Window Easel:** On page 192, you will find plans for a do-it-yourself easel that is easily made from wood and Plexiglas. The clear surface makes a great background for fingerpaint, tempera, or shaving cream paint.

A Note from Lesli

Once your child's fine motor skills have developed and she desires to create art with an intended product in mind, consider replacing the inexpensive art supplies with quality art supplies. She will be able to create what is in her imagination more easily.

• **Think Big!** Tape a large drop cloth over your garage door. Provide your preschooler with poster paints and sponges, and let him make a huge masterpiece! Your kids will have fun throwing the wet paint sponges at the drop cloth. When the art dries, you can use it to protect tables and floors from future crafts.

PRINTING AND STAMPING

Printing and stamping offer preschoolers ways to explore symmetry and develop confidence in their ability to create a picture with accurate size and scale before they are developmentally able to draw it.

• **Fruit Stamping:** Provide a nice selection of fruits cut in half and some edible paint for your child to stamp with. (See the recipe for Edible Fingerpaint on page 64.) Then, he can eat his art!

• **Fingerprint Art:** Ed Emberley has written many wonderful books for children on making art with their fingerprints. In a gallon-size baggie, place a rainbow stamp pad, some paper, one of his books, a pen or pencil, and a small pack of baby wipes. Now you have art on the go!

• **Sink Mat Art**: Inexpensive dollar-store sink mats are great for printmaking. Let your preschooler experiment with different colors of paint and different colors and textures of paper.

MOSAICS AND COLLAGE

- **Magazine Collage:** Children love to cut up magazines and glue the pictures to paper. Your preschooler can make collages of faces, foods, cars, colors, numbers, things that start with specific letters, and so on.
- **Mosaics:** Mosaics differ from collages in that mosaics are pictures created using small pieces of stone, tile, or other materials. Give your preschooler small foam pieces or small tiles, and let her create her own mosaic.
- **Stained Glass Art:** Let your child tear colored tissue paper and stick the pieces to clear contact paper. Cover with another sheet of contact paper, and hang the art in the window.

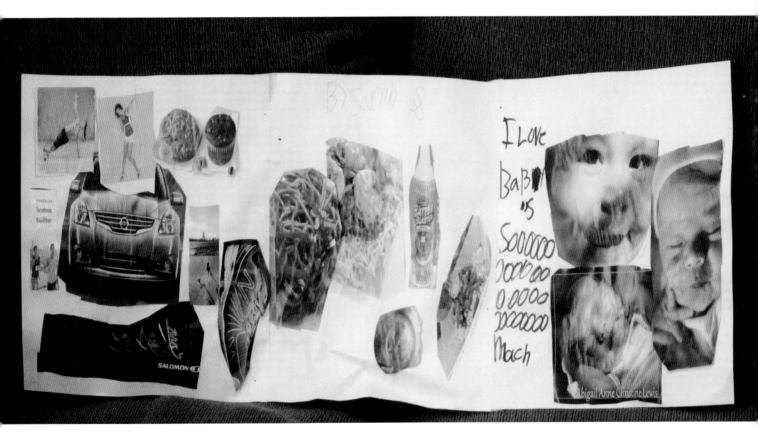

SCULPTURE AND SENSORY ACTIVITIES

Playdough and other sculpting and sensory materials can be used in so many ways! Sculpting is a wonderful, open-ended activity that encourages development in fine motor, language, math, emergent literacy, and social-emotional skills.

Make your own rollers by cutting and sanding large dowels from the hardware store. Provide items to squish into the sculpting medium, such as large buttons, sequins, craft feathers, and beads. Provide alphabet letter and number cookie cutters—you and your child can make names and words together, or cut out numbers and corresponding numbers of shapes. Consider offering a garlic press, safety scissors, straws (for punching holes), leaves, twigs, rocks, birthday candles, and plastic silverware for your child to use.

Preschoolers love to make pretend food out of playdough. Once, Lesli's older daughter made a bakery out of a box with taped-in cardboard shelves and plastic wrap as a window. All day, she and her siblings made cakes, cookies, donuts, and other goodies for Mom and Dad to buy.

- **Aluminum Foil Sculptures:** Give your child a sheet of aluminum foil. He can make snakes, towers, people, robots—anything he can imagine.
- **Sensory Suncatcher:** Squirt hair gel (either colorless with food coloring added or precolored) into a quart- or gallon-size freezer bag. Add fun things for your child to push around within the gel: dried beans, glitter, sequins, buttons, or marbles. Zip the bag closed, and seal it with clear packing tape. Your child will enjoy moving the items around in the bag with his finger, developing his fine motor coordination. If you like, tape the bag to a window at the child's eye level and let the sun shine through the colored gel.
- **Big Dough:** This activity is a fabulous experience for the entire body. Add 1 cup of warm water to 4 cups of white flour, and mix until you have a sturdy dough (add a little more flour if necessary to create a smooth texture). This recipe makes a stretchy dough that is great for sculpting big things: train tracks, a giant pizza, a super-long hot dog, and more.

Quick-Dry Molding Clay

1½ cups baking soda
⅔ cup cornstarch
2 cups warm water

Mix the ingredients together in a pan. Heat over low heat until mixture is thick, stirring constantly. Place mixture on a pastry board or bread board to cool. When clay is cool enough to handle, knead well. At this time you can add tempera paint or food coloring if you choose. Let your child roll the clay out flat. Using cookie cutters or shaping freehand, your preschooler can sculpt whatever she wants. Place unused dough in a plastic bag; it dries fast. Your child can paint her finished projects. When the paint dries, brush with shellac or clear nail polish to preserve (adult only).

● **Clean Mud:** Kathy lovingly refers to this mixture as Fly Guts. Grate two bars of soap (Ivory works well) into a large bucket (adult only). Provide one or two rolls of toilet paper for your preschooler to rip into pieces and add to the bucket. Add enough water to make a thick consistency, similar to mud. Clean mud will take on a life of its own. Vary the consistency to change the activity: Add a little more water and have a thinner consistency for hiding objects or scooping. Another day, make the mixture thicker for building and sculpting. If desired, add a little food coloring or watercolor.

A Note from Kathy

I was at a preschool in Roseville, California, many years ago when a little girl invited me to play with her bucket of fly guts. I realized that we were playing with clean mud, but I've called this activity fly guts ever since!

Lesli's Favorite Playdough Recipe

1 cup water
⅓ cup salt
1 tablespoon vegetable oil

3 tablespoons cream of tartar
food coloring or Kool-aid packets (optional)
lemon or orange extract (optional)

Whisk all ingredients in a medium saucepan until smooth. Cook over medium heat, stirring constantly. The mixture will be lumpy, but it will smooth out and turn darker as you stir. When the mixture forms a ball or lump, remove it from the pan and let cool.

Alternatively, cook this recipe in the microwave on 50 percent power for 5 minutes, stopping every minute to stir. Add food coloring, drink mix powder, or extract if desired. The recipe yields a little over 2 cups of playdough. Store the playdough in the refrigerator in airtight containers.

● **Shaving Cream Paint:** Fill each cup of a six-cup muffin tin with shaving cream. Mix in different food colors, liquid watercolors, or tempera. Your preschooler can use this in the bathtub or on an outdoor easel.

- **Table Time:** Squirt a big blob of shaving cream on your kitchen table, and let your child draw in it. This is simple, but very entertaining! Older children can practice writing letters or numbers or making shapes. Draw a circle, and ask your child to add the details of a happy, sad, or surprised face. Draw half of something, and ask your child to add the other half. This will teach him about symmetry.
- **Puffy Paint Fun:** Add glue to your shaving cream paint for an extra bit of texture. It dries with a different consistency and is fun to feel. This is really fun to use to paint on outlines of pictures of animals.

Sand Dough

2 cups play sand
1 cup cornstarch
½ cup cold water

Mix play sand, cornstarch, and water in a medium saucepan. Stir constantly over medium-low heat for 5–10 minutes until all moisture is absorbed. Remove from heat and let cool.

- **Handprint Sculpture:** Make a batch of sand dough, and place it in a pie tin. Let your child press it out to fill the tin. Encourage her to press her hand firmly in the center of the dough to create her handprint.

Cloud Dough

8 cups flour
1 cup baby oil or vegetable oil
essential oil (optional)
powdered tempera (optional)

Mix flour and baby oil or vegetable oil. If it is too sticky, add more flour. Add essential oils or powdered tempera, if desired. Store in an airtight container.

A Note from Lesli

Our youngest, Rosalie, loves a mess! She's been known to empty entire bottles of shampoo and conditioner on the carpet! On Kathy's advice, I made up a batch of shaving cream paint for her to use in the bathtub; Rosalie's first reactions were fascinating. I gave her a paintbrush, and she delightedly painted the sides of the tub. Then, I modeled fingerpainting with the shaving cream. As blobs of the cream fell into the now colored water, she watched it carefully as it swirled and dissolved, tracing it with her finger. She was completely absorbed in the activity. She kept repeating, "Thank you, Mommy!"

Sensory Table

A sensory table provides a movable surface on which your preschooler can explore all sorts of textures and materials. If you have one that also incorporates a light feature, you can give your child an added dimension of exploration. Consider purchasing a sensory table at school-supply stores or online. Or, we've provided plans for a simple sensory and light table on page 195 in the Appendix.

Safety Note

Many types of commercial birdseed contain capsaicin, the spicy heat in chili peppers, to deter squirrels and other wildlife. Capsaicin is a powerful skin and eye irritant. Look for birdseed that is capsaicin free.

- **Animal Tracks:** Provide an assortment of plastic animals for your preschooler. Encourage him to make animal tracks in the cloud dough. An older child can look at animal tracks in a nature guide and try to mimic them in the dough with his fingers.

- **Wild Animals:** Fill the bottom of a sensory table with pea gravel, some fake plants, and lots of plastic animals. Provide your preschooler with a separate empty bin with a little water in it. Encourage your child to arrange the plants and make habitats for the different animals. This activity is great for sorting, science exploration, and fine motor skill development.

- **Birdseed:** Pour birdseed into the sensory table. Add spoons, measuring cups, and so on for scooping and pouring. Try adding plastic or wooden eggs, clay saucers, bird houses, branches, and toy birds from the floral department of a craft store, so your preschooler can create her own bird habitat. When your child is finished with this activity, use the birdseed to create homemade bird feeders for your yard.

- **Boba Balls:** Boba balls can be found at your local Asian market. These little tapioca gems provide a great sensory experience for your preschooler. Cook according to package directions and cool, then add them to the sensory table. Add items for pouring, scooping, and measuring. For extra fun, add warm water!

- **Black Beans:** Dry beans provide a great sensory material for your preschooler and also make a great "soil" for your child's construction site. Add small construction vehicles, blocks, and play people. Of course, if your child is allergic to peanuts and other legumes, consult your pediatrician before using dry beans.

- **Dirt:** Yes, dirt! Pour some garden soil in the sensory table. (Commercial potting soils can contain additives such as fertilizers that may be harmful to children. Use dirt from your yard instead.) Provide small shovels, dry beans or other seeds, and gardening tools for a fun day of planting. Another day, add some water and let your child make good, old-fashioned mud. Oh, the squeals you will hear!

- **Shredded Paper:** Add shredded paper to the sensory table as a great hide-and-seek material for little treasures.

- **Ice:** Dump several trays of ice (try fun shaped ice trays for extra excitement) into the sensory table. Your preschooler will enjoy building with the blocks and helping the ice to melt. Provide your preschooler with pipettes, beakers, squirt bottles of warm water, and small cups of colored water. This activity will keep going even after the ice is gone.

Brains

8 packets unflavored gelatin
5 ½ cups of boiling water
(adult only)
Empty the gelatin packets
into the boiling water until
completely dissolved. Pour
the gelatin mixture in one
large or two medium plastic
containers. Refrigerate until
gelatin is firm.

Tear It Up: Provide your child with several old magazines, and encourage her to rip to her heart's content. When the sensory table is full of paper shreds, provide a pitcher of water and some tongs. Encourage your child to dump the water into the sensory table and manipulate the wet paper with the tongs. Consider hanging a clothesline for your child to drape her pieces of paper on to dry.

Wheat Berries: Wheat berries offer a unique sensory table experience for a young child. (Of course, if your child is allergic to wheat, has celiac disease, or is gluten intolerant, use a different material.) Provide funnels (make your own from paper), plastic eggs, scoops, and so on, for your child to enjoy.

Water Beads: Children enjoy watching the tiny beads swell up when water is added. Water beads come in a variety of colors, and some even glow in the dark. Water beads are available at floral supply stores and online.

Create a River: Children love to play with rocks; there is something fascinating about the sparkles and shapes. Put about 2 inches of play sand in a sensory table, and fill the table with water, plain or colored. Add some interesting rocks of all shapes and sizes for your child to experience.

It's Snowing: Consider putting instant snow, such as Insta-Snow or SnoWonder, in the sensory table. This product is a polymer that puffs into a fluffy texture when water is added. You can order it online or find it at craft stores. Pull out the scarves and hot cocoa for the full winter effect!

Rice: Uncooked rice has a soothing texture that many young children enjoy. Add plenty of materials for dumping, pouring, and transferring.

- **Brains:** This is a favorite in the Lee household! Dump the gelatin into the sensory table, and provide your preschooler with pipettes and colored water. Watch as he enjoys turning this simple concoction into "brains." If you are up for a wild time, make a triple batch of the brain recipe, and add it to a plastic wading pool. This makes a full-body sensory experience that can be followed with sprinkler play.

- **Doll Bath Time:** Fill the sensory tub with water. Provide your child with some dish soap, a washcloth, a bath towel, and one or two water-safe baby dolls. Encourage your child to wash the dolls; she will be developing social-emotional skills at the same time.

- **Let it Rain:** Children love rain! Create a rain table by punching tiny holes in plastic cups or water bottles with lids, then placing them in a sensory tub full of water. Add a few cups without holes, and watch the children discover that their rain has "stopped." Adding a water wheel to the rain table provides an extension of this idea.

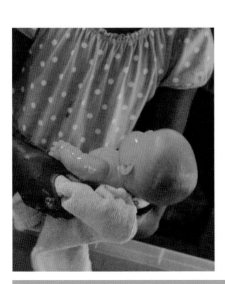

SOCIAL-EMOTIONAL

Field Trip!

Arrange to take your child to visit a local bakery. They can show your child how the treats and breads are made, and you can bring home yummy samples for your family.

At the preschool level, social studies encompasses individual development and identity, a sense of the child's place within the family and community, and learning social skills. We cannot overemphasize the importance of dramatic play in this area. Provide lots of opportunities for your preschooler to explore relationships, interpersonal skills, roles, feelings, and language development through open-ended play.

Some children may need a little inspiration, so if you see that your preschooler struggles in this area, offer some ideas. Lesli's son struggled with pretend play as a preschooler. She found that focusing on pretend play with everyday items such as kitchen sets was easier for him than more imaginative fantasy play.

- **Kitchen:** Play kitchens offer all sorts of learning opportunities. Provide pots and pans, play food, water to pour, utensils, aprons, and chef's hats. Your preschooler can take on different roles, develop vocabulary, even do simple math: "How many people will have dinner? Four? Okay, we will need four forks and four plates." Free plans for building a play kitchen are available at www.ana-white.com.
- **Restaurant:** Use a big appliance box to make a pretend restaurant or ice cream shop. Provide pens and pads for taking orders. Offer aprons and old nametags, cleaning supplies to wipe tables, and play money. Combine the restaurant with the play kitchen and a child's table and chairs to expand this activity.

A Note from Lesli

If you allow your child to put makeup on you, try to catch a glimpse of yourself in the mirror before you head out to run errands, or you may receive some interesting looks!

● **Hair Salon:** Set up a hair salon complete with brushes, combs, empty shampoo bottles, spray bottles, foam curlers, and makeup sets. Make a salon drape out of an old sheet and some Velcro. Let your child pretend to do your hair or a sibling's hair. He can also use dolls and stuffed animals for customers.

- **Post Office:** Make a mailbox together out of a cardboard box decorated with paint or markers and a sign. Then provide paper, envelopes, old address labels, and stickers that resemble stamps. Our children love to make letters for family members and deliver them to their rooms!

- **School:** It is ironic that our homeschooled children love to play school with stuffed animals, dolls, and even Lego people! Little chalkboards, chalk, timers, stickers, lined paper, and crayons are fun props to add to the pretend play. And of course, the students and teacher must have a snack, so provide little paper cups and animal crackers, too.

- **Dress-Up Center:** Offer a wide selection of costumes. If you hit the stores the day after Halloween, you will find all sorts of costumes marked down for a quick sale. If you have a relative or friend who is traveling abroad, ask that person to bring back a child's costume. Ask older girls you know to donate old dance costumes, and add some of your clothes: high heels, bathrobes, shirts, and ties.

- **Tool Time:** Turn a small table into a workshop for your preschooler. Offer blocks of scrap wood and child-size tools. We prefer small real tools to plastic ones, as soon as children are old enough to handle them safely. A preschooler can hammer nails into predrilled wood or golf tees into pegboard. Large blunt bolts and screws are fun to play with as well. Always keep safety in mind, and supervise your preschooler at all times.

- **Doctor's or Vet's Office:** Find costumes and pretend doctor kits after Halloween; turn one of Dad's old dress shirts into a doctor's smock. Provide a small exam table, clean empty medicine bottles, and adhesive bandages. Use stuffed animals or dolls as patients. Cut up an old yoga mat for hospital beds.

- **Fire Station:** Cut an old garden hose to a manageable length, and add a pair of galoshes, an old rain coat, and an inexpensive firefighter helmet to your child's dramatic play costumes. If you pair this activity with a field trip to the local fire station, your child will be inspired to play "fire rescue" for hours!

- **What do you like about _____?** Ask your child about Sunday school teachers, dance teachers, coaches, and family members. Ask her questions such as, What is your favorite memory with _____? What do you think he would love to do this summer?" This is a great activity to do to help you create thank-you gifts. Ask the questions, and use your child's responses to write a thank-you note with your preschooler. Write the words faintly with a pencil, and let your child trace the letters with a marker. Encourage your child to decorate the note.

Dear Mrs. Stephens,
Thank you for being my basketball coach. My favorite thing about this year was when you helped me learn how to dribble the ball. The best thing about being with you is that you always have a happy smile. You are such a good coach, and I hope I have you next year. I hope you get to go to the pool and relax this summer.
Love, Sam

- **Appreciation Window:** Keep a selection of window markers, and let your preschooler dictate "10 Things I Love about Daddy" or "My Sister Is Great Because," or let her draw welcome pictures for a guest. Consider creating a gratitude list with your child, and help her write it on the window.
- **Community Heroes:** Read books to give your child a picture of what community heroes such as firefighters, police officers, medical personnel, lifeguards, or members of the military do. Whenever you see a military person in uniform, thank that person for serving. We have a friend who must leave his family for months at a time to serve tours of duty, and he has commented about how much it means for anyone to notice him and acknowledge his sacrifice.

Field Trip!

Take your preschooler to visit a fire station or police station. Call ahead of time to arrange the visit. Many stations will show children a real fire truck, rescue vehicle, or police car. Some will even let them turn on the siren or wear a real helmet.

A Note from Kathy

Our family enjoys gathering together to sing. My husband and son are musicians, so they lead, and each child takes a turn picking out his favorite song to sing. On one family camping trip with Lesli's family, my husband and some of the kids made up a song called, "Mr. B Has a Burning Hat," about Mr. Richards's hat getting a little too close to the fire. This has become a favorite song for both families.

- **Thankful Jar:** Whenever you find yourself feeling thankful for something, write it down and tell your child about it. By modeling gratitude, you will help your child be more aware of his opportunities to be thankful. Let your child draw pictures to represent things he is thankful for. Place your papers in a jar, and occasionally take them out to review them with your preschooler.

- **Expired Coupon Box:** Did you know that some overseas military bases will accept expired-coupon donations for their personnel? The coupons must be no more than two months past the expiration date, and the donation is not tax deductible. Not all overseas bases will honor the coupons, so check www.ocpnet.org for more detailed information and to sign up. Your preschooler can cut the coupons, put them into envelopes, and mail them herself! With your child, find your adopted base on a map or globe to see where the coupons are going.

- **Family Tree:** With your preschooler, make a list of your family members. Outside, find a fallen tree branch that can serve as your family tree. Secure the branch in a vase, flowerpot, or bucket. Let your preschooler draw and decorate pictures of family members to hang on the tree. Provide yarn, construction paper, and other supplies for gluing on hair, facial features, and clothes for the family members. Punch holes and use ribbon or yarn to tie the family members onto the tree.

- **Body Tracing:** This is a big favorite! Have your child lie down on butcher paper and trace the outline of his body. Let him add facial details, hair, and clothes, and hang the tracing up on his bedroom door.

- **Family Gathering:** Consider starting a family gathering time each morning or evening. You might sing together, tell stories of your day, share journal entries or artwork, or simply cuddle up and read books. Spending time as a family is a great bonding experience for a preschooler; it helps her know she belongs.

- **What Is Your High and Low?** As often as possible, eat dinner together as a family. Consider making dinnertime electronics-free time: no phones, TV, or other electronic devices. Your preschooler can help set the table, pick flowers, or decorate place cards. During the meal, go around the table and let each person share her high event for the day and her low event for the day. You will learn a lot about your family: how they see themselves and what value they place on events in their daily lives.

- **Routine Picture Chart:** It is common to hear a preschooler ask, "What are we going to do today?" To help him know what to expect during the day, create a picture chart of your routine. Have your preschooler decorate a piece of poster board. Label the board, "What Are We Going to Do Today?" Place Velcro adhesive buttons vertically on the left-hand side of the chart. Photograph your preschooler moving through his daily routine: brushing teeth, getting dressed, mealtimes, playing, bath, bedtime. Also take pictures of your child when you are at the grocery store, running errands, visiting the park, or going on a field trip. Hang the poster low on the wall, with a hanging basket next to it. Print the pictures and cover them with clear contact paper. Place Velcro buttons on the backs of the photographs. Each morning, you and preschooler can go through the schedule for that day, and your child can find the picture that matches the activity and place it on the board.

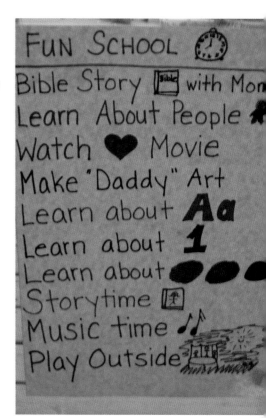

- **Dream Poster:** This is a favorite activity in the Lee home. Furnish every family member with his own poster board. Provide a variety of magazines, glue or tape, and markers. Ask your preschooler (and other family members) to think about what they dream of doing, being, or having. Let them put anything they wish on their posters, and hang the posters in their rooms or display them where the whole family can see them. You will learn a lot about the heart of your preschooler by her dream poster.

- **Family Night:** This can be a movie night, bowling night, game night, craft night—any activity that your family enjoys. Spend time together laughing and talking. Your preschooler will value this time with his family and grow to expect it as part of his weekly routine. Try your best to protect this night and say no to other commitments.

- **Donate It!** When your preschooler outgrows clothes or toys, encourage him to donate them to a specific family or to a local charity. It may be hard for your child to part with some things. In that case, consider making a *Things I Love* book by taking a picture of your child with his special toys and clothes. Talk with your child about how donating toys and clothes will help other families and children.

- **Surprise Someone:** Help your preschooler think of a way to surprise a friend, neighbor, or family member. This can be as simple as taking the neighbor's paper to her door, offering to help a sibling with chores, or making a picture for a friend.

Consider Adopting a Pet

Talk with your family about giving a pet a home. If you can afford the time, energy, and money required to provide a forever home for an animal friend, visit your local animal rescue center to see the pets available in your area. Let your preschooler help with the care of the pet, perhaps helping to feed it and play with it.

- **Volunteer:** Try to involve your preschooler as much as possible in volunteering in your community. For example, if you volunteer at an animal shelter, ask if you can bring your preschooler along to play with the kittens. If you help put together food donations at your church or community center, see if your child can help put the food in bags.

- **Emotion Cards:** Help your preschooler identify his feelings by making emotion cards. Cut large pictures out of magazines that demonstrate a variety of emotions, and glue them onto card stock. Cover these cards with clear contact paper, and tape them to paint stir-sticks to make emotion puppets.

- **A Sad Day:** Help your preschooler identify a lovey or special stuffed animal she can snuggle with on those sad or lonely days. When a sad day comes, bring out the lovey, and read *Alexander and the Terrible, Horrible, No Good, Very Bad Day* by Judith Viorst with your preschooler.

- **I'm So Mad!** Help your child learn that everyone gets angry or frustrated and that there are appropriate ways to express anger. *Hands Are Not for Hitting* by Martine Agassi and *Llama, Llama, Mad at Mama* by Anna Dewdney are great books to read with your child that address the subject of anger. When your child is angry or frustrated, provide a quiet place where she can go and be alone. Sometimes giving her an old magazine to rip up helps get the anger out.

- **Separation Anxiety:** *Owl Babies* by Martin Waddell is a great book that can comfort a child when a loved one is away. If your preschooler does have a parent or loved one who is going away for a time, record that person reading a family favorite book. Play the recording for your child as you read the book together.

- **An App for That:** There are some great apps for electronic devices created to teach children who have special needs or developmental delays. They are useful for typically developing preschoolers as well.

APPENDIX

ACTIVITY CHECKLIST

SUBJECT						MONDAY	TUESDAY	WEDNESDAY	THURSDAY	FRIDAY	WEEKEND
Daily											
Home Life											
Social-Emotional											
Language and Emergent Literacy											
Few Times a Week											
Science											
Gross Motor											
Fine Motor											
Math											
Music											
Art and Sensory											
Once a Week											
Field Trip											

GETTING STARTED CHECKLIST

The following list will help you think about the variety of items you can use to help your preschooler learn and explore. Look around your home—you may be surprised at the number of supplies you already have on hand.

GENERAL

- ❑ calendar
- ❑ CD player/MP3 player
- ❑ cozy reading spot
- ❑ musical instruments
- ❑ audiobooks
- ❑ variety of CDs/downloads
- ❑ weather chart

BLOCKS

- ❑ Duplos or large Legos
- ❑ flat surface for building
- ❑ low shelf or large container or basket
- ❑ small bins of toy cars, trains, wild animals, or small dolls
- ❑ wooden blocks

DRAMATIC PLAY

- ❑ dress-up organizer or large bin
- ❑ dish towels
- ❑ full-length unbreakable mirror
- ❑ kitchen utensils
- ❑ menus
- ❑ placemats
- ❑ play food (and some real empty boxes)
- ❑ play kitchen
- ❑ pots and pans
- ❑ small table and chairs
- ❑ tablet and pencil for taking orders
- ❑ tea set
- ❑ variety of dress-up clothes and hats

MATH AND MANIPULATIVES

- ❑ balance scale
- ❑ beanbags
- ❑ keys and locks
- ❑ lacing cards
- ❑ large beads for stringing
- ❑ large dice
- ❑ magnetic numbers
- ❑ math counters
- ❑ measuring cups
- ❑ measuring tape
- ❑ pattern blocks
- ❑ play money
- ❑ puzzles
- ❑ rulers
- ❑ storage bin for supplies
- ❑ tangrams

LANGUAGE AND EMERGENT LITERACY

- ❑ dry-erase boards
- ❑ journals
- ❑ markers
- ❑ paper in various colors and
- ❑ textures
- ❑ pencil grips
- ❑ pencils
- ❑ pens
- ❑ quality children's books
- ❑ sentence strips

SCIENCE

- ❑ binoculars sensory table or tub
- ❑ light table
- ❑ magnifying glasses
- ❑ materials to explore (shaving cream, sand, shredded paper, and so on)
- ❑ natural items to explore (seashells, rocks, leaves, and so on)
- ❑ nature books
- ❑ nature journals
- ❑ nature table or shelf
- ❑ plastic tablecloth or shower curtain liner for easy cleanup

ART

- ❑ aluminum foil
- ❑ chalkboard
- ❑ child-safe scissors
- ❑ clear contact paper
- ❑ drop cloth
- ❑ easel (freestanding or tabletop)
- ❑ frames, hooks, or corkboard for displaying art
- ❑ glue
- ❑ magazines
- ❑ tape
- ❑ variety of containers for storage
- ❑ variety of paintbrushes
- ❑ variety of papers
- ❑ washable tempera paint
- ❑ watercolors

GROSS MOTOR

- ❑ balls
- ❑ jump rope
- ❑ parachute

FURNITURE, STORAGE, AND EDUCATIONAL SUPPLY RETAILERS

Ana White, www.ana-white.com—Free plans for furniture and lots more!

Art Supplies Direct, www.artsuppliesdirect.com—Offers a large selection of art and educational supplies.

The Container Store, www.containerstore.com—The name says it all.

Discount School Supply, www.discountschoolsupply.com —Everything you need for your art area and more.

Education Works, www.educationworks.com—A great place for math counters, two-sided counters, and so on.

For Small Hands, www.forsmallhands.com—Kitchen and household tools for children.

Fun Science, www.funsciencekits.com—This is a great resource for pipettes, tweezers, color wells, and so on.

IKEA, www.ikea.com—Storage heaven.

Kaplan Early Learning Company, www.kaplanco.com— Huge variety of preschool products, child-sized furniture, light tables, and educational supplies.

Lakeshore Learning, www.lakeshorelearning.com— Preschool products and furniture.

SOURCES FOR CHILDREN'S BOOKS AND EDUCATIONAL RESOURCES

The Book Vine for Children, www.bookvine.com—Retailer of quality children's books.

Evan-Moor, www.evan-moor.com—Publisher of educational resource books.

Gryphon House Books, www.ghbooks.com—Parent resource books and early childhood educational resources, including those by MaryAnn Kohl, Jackie Silberg, Dr. Jean Feldman, and so many more.

Hugh Hanley, www.hughhanley.com—Children's music.

Miss Jackie Music Company, www.jackiesilberg.com— Early childhood music and books.

Turn the Page Press, www.turnthepagepress.com— Children's books and educational resources.

OUR FAVORITE BOOKS (AND ONE DVD)

Bartholomew, Mel. 2006. *All New Square Foot Gardening.* Brentwood, TN: Cool Springs Press.

Barthuly, Lisa. *A Simply Homemade Clean.* Available at www.homesteadoriginals.com.

Bauer, Susan Wise, and Jessie Wise. 2009. *The Well-Trained Mind: A Guide to Classical Education at Home,* 3rd ed. New York: W. W. Norton.

Bortins, Leigh. 2012. *The Core: Teaching Your Child the Foundations of Classical Education.* New York: St. Martin's Press.

Bortins, Leigh. 2007. *Echo in Celebration: A Call to Home-Centered Education.* West End, NC: Classical Conversations.

Brenneman, Kim. 2010. *Large Family Logistics: The Art and Science of Managing the Large Family.* San Antonio, TX: Vision Forum.

Chapman, Gary, and Ross Campbell. 2012. *The Five Love Languages of Children.* Chicago: Northfield.

Dibble, Carole, and Kathy H. Lee. 2000. *101 Easy, Wacky, Crazy Activities for Young Children.* Beltsville, MD: Gryphon House.

Honig, Alice S. 2009. *Little Kids, Big Worries: Stress-Busting Tips for Early Childhood Classrooms.* Baltimore: Paul H. Brookes.

Huff, Mary Jo. 2009. *Storytelling Tips, Techniques, and Tools,* DVD.

Hughes, Daniel A. 2006. *Building the Bonds of Attachment: Awakening Love in Deeply Troubled Children,* 2nd ed. New York: Jason Aronson.

Hunt, Gladys. 2002. *Honey for a Child's Heart,* 4th ed. Grand Rapids, MI: Zondervan.

Kohl, MaryAnn, and Kim Solga. 2008. *Great American Artists for Kids.* Bellingham, WA: Bright Ring. MaryAnn has written more than 20 fabulous art books for young children—we recommend them all! MaryAnn's website is www.brightring.com. Her books are also available through Gryphon House Books.

Kuhn, Kate, ed. 2011. *The Budding Chef.* Silver Spring, MD: Gryphon House.

Laxton, Laura, ed. 2012. *The Budding Artist.* Lewisville, NC: Gryphon House.

Laxton, Laura, ed. 2012. *The Budding Builder.* Lewisville, NC: Gryphon House.

National Geographic. 2001. *My First Pocket Guide: Garden Birds.* Des Moines, IA: National Geographic Children's Books.

National Geographic. 2002. *My First Pocket Guide: Wildflowers.* Des Moines, IA: National Geographic Children's Books.

Patterson, Anice, and David Wheway. 2011. *30 Fun Ways to Learn about Music.* Silver Spring, MD: Gryphon House.

Pica, Rae. 2006. *A Running Start: How Play, Physical Activity, and Free Time Create a Successful Child.* New York: Marlowe.

Purvis, Karyn, David Cross, and Wendy Sunshine. 2007. *The Connected Child: Bring Hope and Healing to Your Adoptive Family.* New York: McGraw-Hill.

Rein, Mary B., ed. 2011. *The Budding Gardener.* Silver Spring, MD: Gryphon House.

Roselli, Stephanie, ed. 2012. *The Budding Scientist.* Lewisville, NC: Gryphon House.

Schiller, Pam, Rafael Lara-Alecio, and Beverly Irby. 2004. *The Bilingual Book of Rhymes, Songs, Poems, Fingerplays, and Chants.* Silver Spring, MD: Gryphon House.

Shelov, Steven, and Tanya Altman. 2009. *Caring for Your Baby and Young Child: Birth to Age 5,* 5th ed. New York: Bantam.

Siegel-Maier, Karyn. 2008. *The Naturally Clean Home: 150 Super-Easy Herbal Formulas for Green Cleaning.* North Adams, MA: Storey Publishing.

Silberg, Jackie, and Pam Schiller. 2002. *The Complete Book of Rhymes, Songs, Poems, Fingerplays, and Chants.* Beltsville, MD: Gryphon House.

Spangler, Steve. 2011. *Fire Bubbles and Exploding Toothpaste: More Unforgettable Experiments that Make Science Fun.* Austin, TX: Greenleaf.

Spangler, Steve. 2010. *Naked Eggs and Flying Potatoes: Unforgettable Experiments that Make Science Fun.* Austin, TX: Greenleaf.

Voskamp, Ann. 2011. *One Thousand Gifts: A Dare to Live Fully Right Where You Are.* Grand Rapids, MI: Zondervan.

West, Sherrie, and Amy Cox. 2001. *Sand and Water Play: Simple, Creative Activities for Young Children.* Beltsville, MD: Gryphon House.

OUR FAVORITE WEBSITES, BLOGS, AND APPS

Art for Small Hands, www.artforsmallhands.com

The Artful Parent, www.artfulparent.typepad.com/ Fabulous art ideas.

Crunchy Betty, www.crunchybetty.com Natural-beauty blog.

Filth Wizardry, www.filthwizardry.com Messy activities for children.

Hands On: As We Grow, http://handsonaswegrow.com

The Healthy Home Economist, www. thehealthyhomeeconomist.com Food and wellness blog.

A Holy Experience, www.aholyexperience.com Ann Voskamp is a homeschool mom who is full of encouragement.

Kididdles, www.kididdles.com Lyrics and music for thousands of children's songs.

Mothers of Preschoolers, www.mops.org Resources and support for mothers of young children.

The National Association for the Education of Young Children, www.naeyc.org An organization dedicated to improving the development and education of young children from birth through age eight.

National Challenged Homeschoolers Associated Network, www.nathhan.com Support for homeschooling families with children who have special needs.

Play at Home Mom LLC, http://playathomemom3. blogspot.com

Tammy Glaser, http://home.earthlink. net/~tammyglaser798/authome.html Tammy runs the Aut-2-Be-Home web ring for bloggers who are homeschooling children who have autism.

Elmo Loves ABCs, app teaches letter recognition.

Feed Me! Pencilbot Preschool, app lets child feed correct answers to a monster.

Intro to Math by Montessorium, app teaches preschool math skills.

iTouchiLearn Feelings for Preschoolers at http:// staytoooned.com.

iWriteWords, app teaches child to write letters, numbers up to 20, and simple words.

Monkey Preschool Lunchbox, app teaches matching, counting, comparison, and letter recognition.

SuperWhy! ABC Adventures, app teaches letter recognition, letter sounds, and letter writing.

Instructions for DIY Plexiglas Easel

Materials

One 30" x 36¼" x ¼" sheet
    Plexiglas
Six 1" x 4" x 8' pine furring strips
Four 1" x 1" x 8' pine furring strips
One 2" x 4" x 8' pine stud
One 1" x 10" x 4' pine board
Wood glue
Sandpaper (80, 150, and 220 grit)
10-year deck stain or exterior paint

Tools

Pocket-hole jig
1¼" coarse-thread pocket-hole screws
    or 1¼" or 2" drywall screws
Paint-grade pocket-hole plugs (or
    wood filler if using drywall screws)
Orbital sander
Miter saw
Drill
Pneumatic nailer
Painter's tape
Economy-grade paint brush
Drop cloth

Cut List

Frame top: 1" x 4" x 37½"
Frame sides (two): 1" x 4" x 46½"
Frame bottom: 1" x 4" x 36¼"
Plexiglas strips (two): 1" x 1" x 36¼"
Plexiglas strips (two): 1" x 4" x 30"
Feet (two): 2" x 4" x 24"
Frame supports (two): 1" x 4" x 10½" (long side, cut on 45 degree angle)
Paint holder (two): 19" x 7½" (cut at half of an oval)
Top holder support (two): 2" x 4" x 1½"
Bottom holder support (two): 2" x 4" x 4"

How to Do It

1. Sand the furring strips using an orbital sander and 80-grit sandpaper.
2. Using a miter saw, cut all pieces except for the Plexiglas strips. Note: Keep the protective coating on the Plexiglas while you are working on it, to keep it from being dinged or marked up during construction. We cut the paint holder using a 19" x 14" turkey platter as a template. We cut four 3¼" holes, which fit four 1-pint, large-mouth mason jars.
3. Drill pocket holes into the frame sides using measurements indicated by the pocket-hole jig. Remember that the furring strips are ⅝" thick. If you are using 2" drywall screws instead of a pocket-hole jig, drill pilot holes countersunk just below the face of the board so that the wood does not split when you tighten the screws.
4. Attach the frame top to the frame sides so that the outside face of the frame sides is flush with the end of the frame top.
5. Drill pocket holes into the bottom face of the frame bottom, or if you are using drywall screws, drill pilot holes so that the wood will not split when you tighten the screws.
6. Attach the frame bottom to the inside of the frame sides so that the top face of the frame bottom is 30" from the bottom face of the frame top.
7. Attach the feet to the frame sides. (Hint: Use scrap wood such as 1" x 1" x 3½" to keep the feet stable while you attach the frame supports.)
8. Drill pocket holes into the bottom edge only of the frame supports. Place the supports so that the two long sides form a point in the middle of the frame side. If cut properly, the frame supports will form a triangle with the feet. Attach the frame supports to the frame sides using 1¼" drywall screws.
9. Attach the frame supports to the feet using pocket-hole screws or 2" drywall screws.
10. Cut the Plexiglas strips using a miter saw; cut them to fit inside the frame. If you do not want to bother with miter cutting, cut your Plexiglas strips 2"

Easel

NOTE: All measurements are in inches.

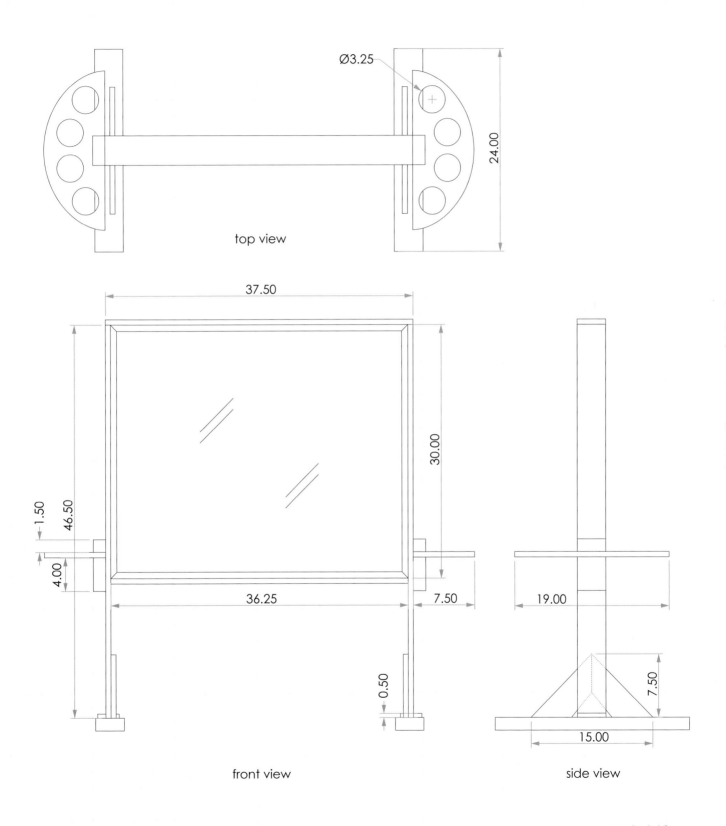

top view

Ø3.25

24.00

37.50

30.00

1.50

46.50

4.00

36.25

7.50

0.50

19.00

7.50

15.00

front view

side view

scale 1:10

(CONTINUED)

shorter than the sides of the Plexiglas (24" and 34"). The idea here is that the Plexiglas needs to be in the center of the frame. If the Plexiglas is ¼" thick and the frame is 3½" wide, then the inside edge of the Plexiglas strip is 1⅝" from the edge of the frame. If the Plexiglas strip is 1" wide, then the outside edge of the Plexiglas strip is ⅝" from the edge of the frame.

11. Attach the Plexiglas strips using a pneumatic nailer. Attach the strips to only one side of the frame. Peel the protective coating far enough away from the edge of the Plexiglas sheet so that it doesn't get stuck behind the strip. Insert the Plexiglas.

12. Once that is seated, repeat the process on the other side, only this time you won't need to measure—just press the strip against the Plexiglas and nail in place.

13. Attach the bottom holder support to the outside face of the frame side so that the top edge is 17¼" up from the top of the feet. Glue and screw into place.

14. Place the paint holder on top of the bottom holder support so that it is centered with the frame side, using glue between the bottom holder support and paint holder.

15. Attach the top holder support to the frame side using glue and screws, while firmly sandwiching the paint holder. Be sure that there is glue between the top holder support and the paint holder.

16. Tape the edges of the Plexiglas to protect the surface from scratches. Sand the wooden parts of the easel with 150-grit sandpaper. Then, sand with 220-grit sandpaper.

17. Stain or paint the easel to protect it from the elements.

INSTRUCTIONS FOR DIY LIGHT TABLE OR SENSORY/SAND AND WATER TABLE

This set of plans can be adapted easily for use as a sensory table, sand and water table, or a light table.

CUT LIST

Tabletop: (one) 24" x 48" plywood

End rails: (two) 1" x 4" x 22"

Side rails: (two) 1" x 4" x 44¾"

Center support: (one) 1" x 3" x 20¾"

Table legs: (four) 1" x 4" x 21¾"

Stringer support: (two) 1" x 4" x 19½"

Stringer: (one) 1" x 4" x 41½"

Clear plastic cover (light table): (one) 18" x 24"

HOW TO DO IT

1. Cut the plywood to 48" x 24."

2. Sand the edges with an orbital sander and 80-grit sandpaper. Slightly round the corners to prevent splinters and chipping.

3. Measure and mark the size(s) of the opening(s) needed to accommodate the tubs. Using a circular saw, cut straight lines, and then use a sabre saw to cut the rounded corners. (Tip: To get the rounded corners, we used a 3¼-ounce spice can.)

4. Sand the edges and the corners as you did in step 2. Make sure that you account for any tabs or lip edges on the tubs. To ensure that the top lip fits securely on the table surface, you may need to cut notches in the table.

5. Sand the furring strips with an orbital sander and 80-grit sandpaper.

6. Cut the rest of the table parts using a miter saw.

7. Set the tabletop upside down on a pair of sawhorses. This will be a work surface as you assemble the rest of the table. Drill the pocket holes into the side rails using the measurements indicated by the jig. Remember that your furring strips are actually ⅝" thick. Attach the side rails to the end rails so that the outside face of the side rail is flush with the end of the end rail. If you will not be using a pocket-hole jig, then attach the end rails to the side rails using 2" drywall screws. Remember to drill pilot holes that are countersunk just below the face of the board so that the wood doesn't split when you tighten the screws.

8. If you are building the sand and water table, attach the center support to the midpoint of the side rails, at approximately 22⅜." If you are building the light table, where the hole passes the midway point, simply attach the center support so that it is 1–2" from the edge of the hole.

9. Drill the pocket holes into the center support. If you will not be using a pocket-hole jig, then you can attach the center support to the side rails by

MATERIALS

One 4' x 8' x ¾" pine sanded plywood (one side looks nice; the other may have knot holes)

Plastic tubs:

- For the light table, one 15¼" x 21¾" x 6"
- For the sand and water table, two bins (make sure one side of each tub is smaller than 19½," so it will fit between the table legs
- For sensory table, you can use one bin or two

Eight 1" x 4" x 8' pine furring strips

One 1" x 3" x 8' pine furring strip

1¼" pocket-hole screws, coarse thread, or 1¼" or 2" drywall screws

Paint-grade pocket-hole plugs or wood filler

Wood glue

Sandpaper (80 grit, 150 grit, and 220 grit)

10-year deck stain or exterior paint

Plastic primer (spray)

Reflective silver spray paint

String of lights (for the light table)

One sheet of clear plastic, 18" x 24" (for the light table)

TOOLS

Orbital sander

Circular saw, Sabre saw, and Miter saw

Sawhorses or other firm work surface

Pocket-hole jig

Jigsaw with small, fine-tooth blade

Drill

Speed square

Economy grade paintbrush

Drop cloth

using 2" drywall screws. Remember to drill pilot holes that are countersunk just below the face of the board so that the wood doesn't split when you tighten the screws.

10. Attach each table leg to the inside face of the side rail, making sure it is tight against the end rail. You may want to use a speed square to ensure that the leg is perpendicular to the side rail. Use wood glue and secure with 1¼" drywall screws.

11. Attach the stringer support into the table legs using pocket holes drilled into the inside face of the stringer support. If you will not be using a pocket-hole jig, then you can attach the stringer support to the table legs by putting screws through the outside face of the table leg and into the end of the stringer support. Use wood glue and 2" drywall screws.

12. Mark the center of the stringer support (should be at 9¾"). Be sure to align the center of the stringer (the ⁵⁄₁₆" mark) with the center of the stringer support. Attach the stringer using pocket holes drilled into the back side face of the stringer. If you will not be using a pocket-hole jig, then attach the stringer support directly to the stringer using glue and 2" drywall screws.

13. Drill pocket holes in the side rails (about five on each) and end rails (three). Be sure that all sides are 1" from the outside face of the rails. If you will not be using a pocket-hole jig, then you will need to attach the tabletop to the table base by going through the tabletop into the rails. This is a bit tricky because you will need to make sure you get into the side of the rail, which is only ⅝" thick.

14. Sand the entire table with 150-grit sandpaper, and then sand with 220-grit sandpaper.

15. Paint the table with exterior paint, or stain the table with 10-year deck stain.

16. For the sand and water table or sensory table, drop in the tubs and fill with whatever materials your children would like to explore: sand, water, shaving cream, dry beans, dry rice, and so on.

17. For the light table, spray the inside of one of the bins with plastic primer, following the directions on the can, and let dry. Spray the inside of the bin with silver reflective paint, following the directions on the can, and let dry.

18. Cut a hole (for example, 1⅜") in the side of the bin (big enough so that a string of lights will fit through).

19. Cut the plastic cover for the light table. Keep the protective coating on while you work, to avoid scratches during the cutting and sanding process. Cut the corners using a jigsaw with a very small fine-tooth blade. If you need to trim one of the sides to fit your particular bin, use a sharp utility knife and a straight edge, making several passes until the cut is deep enough to simply snap the piece off.

20. Use 150-grit sandpaper to sand all the edges.

21. Thread the string of lights through the hole in the bin, and connect to a power source.

Table

NOTE: All measurements are in inches.

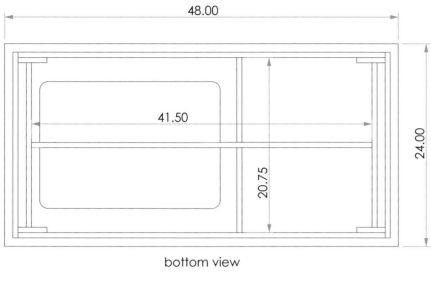

bottom view

top view

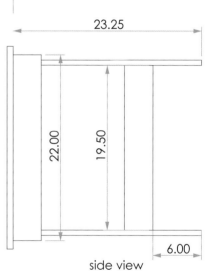

side view

front view

scale 1:10